The Horror of 1888

The Horror of 1888

The True Story
of the Crime, Escape, and Capture
of John Kuehni

Betty Plombon

atmosphere press

This book is dedicated to the many Kuehni family members from the past who gave me much joy as I dug deep into old records, microfilms, foreign records, and newspapers. It is also dedicated to those who corresponded with me from about 1980 to the present, helping me gather the material necessary to put this book together.

However, many of those ancestors from long ago created enormous challenges for me. They made my hunt much harder, as they left records in foreign languages I could not read, gave census takers incorrect birthdates, and gave their children the same first names as the generation before them, all of which made the game more challenging. Many managed to keep themselves out of newspapers and books, were not home when the census taker arrived, and otherwise hid from my research.

Some even broke the law, giving me my greatest problem: How do I handle great-great-uncle John? I attacked that problem by deciding that John would probably not be the last to create such a problem for me and to simply tell the truth and carry on.

Introduction

I am a historical researcher turned writer. My forty-plus years of research into this story has been both exciting and rewarding. When I began, I was not looking for lawbreakers, but I found some anyway, including one I really did not want to find.

Orin Parker, writing for *Ancestry* in 2003, shared my sentiment when he said, "In the beginning, I was certainly not looking for lawbreakers, but no matter how I may wish them away, I have found some. Perhaps I was looking for royalty; it would have been nice to find a court jester, or two, but that did not happen."

This book, *The Horror of 1888*, gives an accurate account of a horrible murder that took place in southern Wisconsin in December of 1888. The story is about John Kuehni/Kuhni, a member of my family on my mother's side, and has lain hidden in our family for over 130 years. I know my relatives at that time would have liked to have this story forever erased from history, but due to the vast amount of contemporary newspaper coverage, this would never happen. My ancestors, living in stiff-backed, nineteenth-century Wisconsin, drew a veil of embarrassment over the event for many years.

If I had not researched and published this story, someone, someday, would have found the material and put a story together. A few articles have already been published, but they do not contain all the details I have made available in this publication—details that help us understand why John did the deed.

Once I decided to look into my family history, I asked my mother some questions about her ancestors in the Kuehni family, and her answer was, "If you continue to dig into this family, you will find things you do not want to know about. Do not do it!"

When pushed further, she vaguely remembered a story told to her about someone being killed and thrown overboard during immigration, or something like that, she said; she was not sure about anything. She stammered and continued: "They say that a great-uncle of mine murdered someone—or he was murdered—or something happened on the boat to America when he emigrated."

She could not or would not recall anything more.

She left me hanging with no dates, no names, just a great desire to find out more about this story—a family story she did not want me to know anything about.

I next asked some of her cousins, who lived in the Madison area, if they could give me some information about the story, and they told me they had heard some tales and had read something about it in the newspapers, but it was the same information my mother had given me, which was very little. I could tell they were being cautious and wanted to cover something up, something that must not come to light.

What more to whet someone's appetite. I was hooked! I was off and running. I was not about to forget about it. Just the idea that someone in my dull-as-dishwater family might have done something atrocious was all it took to push me forward, and I knew then that it was up to me to find out precisely what happened, to get the facts straight and to unpuzzle the mystery.

I wanted to know more about John Kuehni, who was supposed to have done something horrible, and I needed more information to reconstruct the story. More than one hundred years of tangled myths and false information was keeping me from the facts.

It took me about a year to even find the year the event happened. The first clue came from a reference index to a John Kuhni in the Madison papers, which helped pull this story together. Newspapers were not indexed when I began this story; I had to do it the hard way.

From then on, what I learned was far better than the many years of family silence and shame. That was forty-plus years ago, and I am still finding material about this story. I write this to inform my line of Kuehni descendants and any interested readers about a story that has been hushed in our family for many years, and to help them to understand how an ancestor of ours could have possibly done such a horrendous deed. There is still missing information that will probably never come to light because private legal and medical records were destroyed. However, the satisfaction of having found what I did compels me to tell you, the reader, the real story.

This book reads like a novel—it has a beginning, a middle, and an end—except that everything is true and documented. Rather than merely relating historical facts, I have placed the story within its historical setting by using material from many newspaper articles, along with the court transcripts. Woven into the story are facts pertaining to the Kuehni family, and the social, ethnic, and local history of the area at the time.

Now that many members of the last two generations of the Kuehni family who remembered parts of this stormy story have passed on, I will attempt to present it in a way that can be understood by those who remain. Today, about 99 percent of the family still do not know anything about this man lurking in the background of their ancestry. They will be shocked by what they read.

I know that our ancestors, who were very embarrassed by John during their lifetimes, will be turning over in their graves once this book is published, and I will probably be condemned.

Be sure to read entirely through to the end, because a very unusual reason for the murder is revealed in the final pages.

The name in Wisconsin today is spelled "Kuehni." I will use the spelling Kuhni in this story as this is how the papers spelled it in nineteenth-century Wisconsin. I will spell it this way for this story only.

Every family has a scoundrel or a black sheep, or even two if we dig deep enough. As George Bernard Shaw once said, "If you cannot get rid of the family skeleton, you may as well make it dance." So, I decided to flesh out that skeleton in my family, deal with it, and make it dance!

Chapter One
Body Found

It was the month of December, and Christmas Day would be celebrated on a Tuesday this year. Friday, December 21, when people were finishing their Christmas shopping in nearby Madison or in other small towns, was an unusually warm day. It was the kind of day you notice just before the "blast" we are accustomed to in Wisconsin. Only two days later, a cold front would move in, bringing subzero temperatures and lots of frigid wind. By December 23, it would be forty-five degrees below zero, and the roads would be very unstable with drifts of snow and ruts filled with ice and mud, as roads were not paved at that time.

On this Friday before Christmas, brothers George and William Rea, of Springdale, decided to take advantage of what would probably be the last warm day until spring by going fishing on the West Branch of the Sugar River. The northern section of Primrose Township is watered by the West Branch and two of its tributaries. The Winnebago Indians, who previously fished her waters and hunted her lands, named the river the Sugar River. Its headwaters are located northeast of Mount Horeb. The river snakes its way south through pastures and croplands and has always been a popular fishing river.

The brothers were fishing only about one hundred rods away from the Holland Cheese Factory. It was a quiet day, and it felt warmer than the thermometer showed. Cows grazed along the creek, which runs west to east at this point. The men were dressed in short-sleeved shirts with no jackets.

George had worked his way up the crystal-clear stream to a part of the river that was only two to three feet deep, and only six inches deep in places. Walking along the edge of the stream, he noticed a gunnysack in the water. "Hey, William, come and help me get this sack out of the water. Let's see what's in it," he yelled.

Laying down his pole, William walked over to where his brother was waiting and reached down to help him lift the feed sack out of the water. The bank was shallow, and the sack was easy to get out, even though it was quite bulky. After fishing it out onto the bank, William turned it over. "That's funny," he said. "The sack is too heavy to have floated here. Someone must have left it here, but why? Maybe we should not be disturbing it; they may come back for it."

They both stood looking down at the soaked bag and wondering how it could have gotten there. Why would anyone leave a sack in the water? It could not have floated down from somewhere, as the river was too shallow at this point, and the bag too heavy. One brother said, "Feels like there might be a jug in it." Then temptation overcame them, and William, not willing to wait any longer, ripped the bag open and out tumbled—a man's head, liver, and intestines. Stepping back, William managed a few words: "Well, lookee here. I believe this belongs to the body of a person."

The bag also contained a pair of wooden shoes and a stone, which had obviously been added to weigh the sack down. At first, they were not able to say much as they silently studied the remains of a man and the face of a stranger. Actually, they were struck dumb, with horrible thoughts flooding their minds. After regaining some composure and discussing what they should do next, it was decided that William would leave the remains with his brother, George, and go for help. William scurried off to the nearest home, located north of the factory, occupied by N. N. Byrge.

It took a while to locate Mr. Byrge, who was away from his house and when found needed to finish the job he was doing at the time before being escorted to the creek scene. Byrge immediately recognized and identified the face in the sack as that of William Christen, who lived and worked at the Holland Cheese Factory, only a few rods from where they stood. After discussing what to do, the three men carried the remains to the cheese factory.

The owners of the factory, Mr. Holland and Mr. Gruening, were called in and confirmed that the remains were those of Christen. The sack and its contents were left in their care, and the two fishermen returned to their home. It was getting late, and they needed to get home to clean their catch for supper. Their mother was waiting to fry the fish for them.

Someone then jumped on a horse and went to notify Justice Ole Barton, who lived about one and a quarter mile to the northwest. After Barton arrived at the factory and examined the remains, the Honorable P. O. Baker arrived as well, and also identified the remains as William Christen, remarking, "This looks like it could only be murder. Who could have done such a thing, and why?"

Ole Barton was a farmer in the town of Primrose and the town chairman at this time, having served on the board since 1871. Barton had organized the first cooperative cheese factory in Primrose. He was born in Norway, taught in local schools, served in the Civil War, and had been farming for forty years in Primrose. He was one of the most respected men in the area.

The men discussed what each of them knew about Christen, and it began to dawn on them that John Kuehni, Christen's roommate, was not around. Where was he, and why wasn't he there?

Nils Holland told the group that on December 13, 1888, at six or seven in the evening, Peter Sangesand and himself were concerned about a large amount of smoke coming from the cheese factory with a peculiar smell, like hair or meat burning. They walked to the factory, located only yards from their homes. They knew John Kuehni and William Christen worked there as cheesemakers. Peter, a young man in his twenties, was working part-time for A. S. Holland. Nils was a son of Mr. Holland. The Hollands lived just south of the factory.

As the two men approached the door of the factory, they'd called out, "Hello-Hello, what's wrong here?"

John Kuehni, coming to the door, implied that everything was all right. Not satisfied with this answer and still concerned about the smell of smoke, they went around to the outside cellar door and found it locked. They yelled for John to come and open that door, which he did.

They first entered the milk room, which at first looked good to them, and then went into the salting room, where they also found everything OK. As they entered the main cellar, they discovered the reason for the smell and the smoke. Here they found a fire on the dirt floor. John immediately told them that everything was all right. He had the fire under control, and there was no reason for them to worry. They reminded him to be careful with the coals and asked where Christen was. John replied, "He is about somewhere." They left without giving much more thought to the incident.

⌒

One of the investigators suggested going to the home of John's brother, Fritz Kuehni, to ask about John. Perhaps John would be found there and could explain some things. Someone mounted a horse and traveled the mile and a half to Fritz Kuehni's home. They discovered that John was not there, but Fritz offered to accompany the messenger to the factory to help.

As Fritz traveled to the factory, he had time to think about a previous morning when he had taken his brother to the railroad station in New Glarus. What had John told him that morning? He tried to recall all they had discussed, and some of the conversations slowly began to come back to him. He realized things did not add up quite right about that morning and about what John had told him.

When Fritz arrived at the factory, he was shown the evidence from the sack that had been found in the river. After listening to the information, the men provided, he replied, "No one, but my brother could have done this deed!"

At 4 p.m. Justice Barton appointed a coroner's jury to investigate further, and most of the men returned to their homes knowing they would be back the next morning to join the investigation.

⌒

Fritz Kuehni and someone else spent the night in the factory with the remains of the body, which was wrapped in rags, according to the report filed later.[1] I find this hard to believe, as Fritz would have needed to inform his wife of what was going on. There were no telephones at the time to call her, and with no word as to his whereabouts, she would have been anxious and concerned when he did not return. He would have had chores to do, animals to care for. Also, there was no place to sleep in the factory and no food. With all the blood spilled around the only livable room, it would have been hard to find a clean place to lay their heads down. They would also not have wanted to disturb any evidence before the investigation and trial, which was to take place the next day.

If the two did stay the night, I doubt either got much sleep. Nightmares would have been frequent throughout that long night. The shock of seeing the horror that one human being could inflict upon another would linger in their minds for years, perhaps throughout their lifetimes, especially for Fritz Kuehni.

---

[1] Info taken from various articles in the *Wisconsin State Journal* and the *Madison Democrat*

Chapter Two
The Ghastly Sight

An examination called a Coroner's Examination, began the following morning, undertaken by the jury appointed the day before. Eli Pederson, Martin Hobbs, Gutlick Anonson, K. P. Myrland, P. O. Baker, John Tascher, and, of course, Justice Barton served on this jury. Others were present out of curiosity, along with Fritz and the neighbor boys. All had traveled to the factory on horseback or by horse and buggy on a cold, gloomy, rainy day. Everyone knew each other, as they were all farmers from the area, and most had served on the town board of directors and other government committees. Dr. S. Johnson, of Mount Vernon, arrived shortly after being called in to examine the body parts.

In cases of a suspected criminal killing, the role of the jury is to decide whether to commit a person to stand trial. This jury does not convict a person of an offense but accuses him of the alleged assault and makes him stand trial. In this case, the panel was to look for clues and decide who should be hunted down by the local authorities.

When a person dies suddenly, a coroner will be called. The coroner conducts an inquest into the manner or cause of death and confirms the identity of the person who has been found dead. Any coroner at that time would have had absolutely no medical schooling at all. Most were local persons who were forced to take the job, as most people did not want it. The coroner could have been a store clerk, a funeral director, or anyone willing to take the job. Many coroner exams were done in a storeroom or such, with very few instruments and little cleanliness.

By this time in history, the office of coroner had a reputation for corruption. A bribed coroner could help cover up a murder. He could also help a rich and/or powerful family avoid public embarrassment when a relative committed suicide. Coroners could easily paper over a mob hit, or exonerate a parent of child abuse.

∾

The cheese factory was a one-story, wood-framed building with a deep cellar built along a hillside. It was essential to have the building located against a hill so that the building's backside would be kept cool. A creek ran west to east in front of the factory. A good water supply, either from a spring, a creek, or a deep well, was necessary for any factory. Almost every factory had a few rooms added to it for living space for the cheesemaker or for another employee.

Local farmers, as they brought in loads of milk to sell, would drive their wagons across the creek from the south and turn right to enter the unloading dock of the factory. Cheese factories at that time were small and served only about five or six farmers each, as they were not big enough to handle more milk. The farmers had to deliver their milk to the factory, by horse and wagon, at a certain time each morning. They were unable to travel very far by horse.

The jurors entered the factory to begin their investigation. Some had seen the remains the day before, but every item and clue had to be gone over again for those who had just arrived that morning so that each man would understand the circumstances. After searching the actual factory where the cheese was made and noticed nothing unusual, the men moved into the living quarters. Someone had made a fire in the stove hoping to make the search a little more comfortable for the men but the room remained cold from the dampness outside. Wisconsin winters are brutal, and the building was built to be a cheese factory, not a comfortable home.

Shivering, the men began to look around, wondering to themselves how Kuhni and Christen could have lived here; it was so primitive, dirty, and cold. However, the two immigrants from the mountains of Switzerland were used to cold climates. They had survived in the past, and they had survived here.

Partitioned off in a corner on the first floor was a small bedroom where the two men had evidently slept together, sharing one bed. The walls in this room were splattered with blood.

In 1888, little was known about the behavior of blood. Blood is not like any other liquid, and when a person's arteries are cut, it does not drip or slowly drain away. The resulting splatter can be found very high up on any nearby wall.

"Perhaps the deed had been done here," someone declared. The walls looked as though someone had attempted to wash the stains off, with very poor results. It was also evident the walls had been rubbed with ashes to hide the stains, and some bloodstained clothes that looked as if they had been used in an attempt to clean the walls were strewn around the room. The floor was covered with ashes and litter to hide the great pools of blood. Rugs were pulled back, revealing more bloodstains.

Dr. S. Johnson was asked to examine the body parts. He stated that the head had been severed from the body by an oblique cut extending from the middle of the right ear to the lower jaw on the left side. There were six cuts on the scalp and forehead, evidently made by an ax. The liver had several cuts in it, but the intestines and spleen were in such a bad state of deterioration that he could not satisfactorily examine them.

After the examination, the party went outside to enter the downstairs through the outside cellar door. As the men passed the shambles of a door that led down into darkness, they soon noticed a terrible odor from the cellar. A lantern was quickly found, causing the men's shadows to leap high against the walls. The illumination from the lantern immediately began to intensify their other senses, especially smell. The fetid, dank air hung heavy, and all wondered if they really wanted to see what was down there.

Thank goodness for Justice Ole Barton, a true professional. Most of the people appointed to this jury wanted out of there, but Barton had a feeling this dark, oppressive place held something they needed to see and was probably where the real business had been done. It was too dark to see very much, and soon another lantern arrived to provide more illumination. The men began to shiver even more as it was very damp and cold in the cellar, as the small amount of heat from the stove upstairs did not reach this underground area at all.

Peering at the scene before them, the men began to murmur among themselves. They stopped moving forward, running their hands through their hair, stunned into silence at the mess they had found. The place was dreadfully dirty, and spoiled cheese added to the cellar's unpleasant smell. Some looked a little sick to their stomach, turning their heads back toward the entrance and wondering if they could make it outside in time. Someone, evidently with a strong stomach, called out, "Over here, I found something," moving the men into action.

An ax had been found, covered with hair and blood clear up to the handle. It also had been rubbed with ashes, probably to cover the blood. Behind some shelves was found a part of a bed tick, stained with what was most likely the lifeblood of Christen. On a wooden tub was found hair, which appeared to be human, and more blood. It was soon assumed the tub had been used to chop up the body. A large stick of wood, generously covered with blood and hair, was found in the carpenter's room. A pair of bloody, wet overalls and a vest were also discovered.

These items were retained by Justice Barton and later given to District Attorney John Erdall. A large trunk appeared to have been broken into, as its contents were scattered about.

The men were stunned and confused. No one on the scene had ever seen anything this disturbing before. Some thought: Could one man have done all this, or could more than one person have been involved? Today, we might describe it as being like a movie scene, but they, in 1888, had never experienced movies. They also had not experienced television like we do today, where our eyes have viewed just about every horrible or hard-to-believe thing imaginable. For these men, at this time, the scene was more than they could understand. The closest thing they had ever seen was the butchering of animals on their farms.

The search continued for the remainder of the body, but nothing was found except some small bones and pieces of cloth in the ashes of the fire on the cellar floor that had created the smoke and smell on the thirteenth. (The bones were later proved to be from a small animal, such as a rabbit or squirrel.)

After listening to testimony from the owners of the factory, the doctor, several neighbors, the two men who had seen smoke coming from the factory several days before, and John Kuehni's brother, Fritz, the jury decided that Christen had come to his end by the foul deeds of his partner, John Kuehni, who appeared to be missing.[2]

After much discussion about the motive for such an act, they determined that Kuehni must have been after the money that had just been paid to Christen, probably $300 to $400, for his summer and fall work.

It was determined that Christen had died sometime from December 12 to December 14 and that Kuehni had spent the day following the murder attempting to clean the crime scene and dispose of the body. Kuehni, they decided, had probably left the area on the fourteenth.

Justice Barton's report:

We, the jury, after reviewing the testimony, have ruled that William Christen came to his death between December 12 and 14, 1888, by some sharp instrument in

---

[2] *Madison Democrat,* 24 Dec. 1888

the hands of John Kuhni.

Each member of the jury signed his name: Eli Pederson; P. O. Baker; Martin Hobbs; John Tascher; and Knudt Pederson. Then Justice Barton signed and dated it. Barton then left to file the report in Madison, the county seat.

Sangesand, Fritz Kuehni, and an unknown cheesemaker decided to place the mortal remains in a wooden box and bury them in the Holland graveyard. (The Holland graveyard has never been located, and therefore it is today unknown where Christen's remains were actually interred.)

There was no taking the remains to a funeral director for burying. Was there no family to accept the remains? No funeral plans, and nowhere for the curious to gather and talk about what happened, as after most tragedies? Nothing has ever surfaced for answers to these questions.

I have also been unable to find much information about the deceased, William Christen or his family. There was a Wilhelm Christen, age 26 (born about 1860), in Switzerland, who arrived in the United States on April 13, 1885, at the Port of New York. His occupation was listed as a farmer, and he evidently traveled without family, as no one else on the ship had the name Christen. This could be the person who was killed. It is strange that there was never a memorial service held for him, no death certificate, no other record of him. There is just no further information about this man.

Chapter Three
Fritz Enters the Scene

Fritz Kuehni, brother to John, was among those who carefully examined the evidence. He reportedly had spent the night in the cheese factory building and still was having a difficult time keeping his stomach down, even though he had not eaten any breakfast, for the same reason.

After the examination and the burial, as everyone is leaving, Fritz also prepares to leave for home. But first, he stops and takes a deep breath. The horror of what must have happened starts to become real to him. As his eyes search the countryside and the far horizon, a feeling of extreme fatigue, of a great depression, settles over him. The emotional strain and lack of sleep begin to take hold.

He knows in his heart that it was his brother, John, who had done this evil deed. But why had he done it in such a horrible way? Nothing Fritz can comprehend will explain this. What will he tell his parents back in the old country? Will anyone even believe the details of this gruesome story?

As he continues to gaze across the fields and the woods behind him, he shakes his head. He still cannot believe what he has just encountered. However, he knows that the others on that makeshift jury believed. They had seen the head, the body parts, the blood, the ax. They had smelled the horrible smell of decay. They certainly believed it.

He begins to recall a previous night when his brother

arrived at his house.

✑

No document remains to tell us exactly what happened the night of December 14, 1888, in the township of Primrose, Wisconsin, at the home of Fritz Kuehni. However, it is not hard to imagine that something such as this probably occurred:

Fritz was coming out of a sound sleep as someone pounded on the door of his humble log cabin. It was three-thirty in the morning. Someone pounding on the door so late at night probably meant something was wrong, or someone seriously needed help. He jumped from the bed onto the ice-cold bare floor. The night was freezing, cold, and dark, and his fire had gone out several hours before. His wife also was awake and concerned, grabbing a wrap as she, too, rose from the bed. She also knew something was wrong, as there were very few people who traveled the road in front of their house, even in daytime hours. Perhaps someone needed shelter from the cold.

As Fritz was pulling on his trousers over the long underwear he wore to bed, he recognized the voice of his brother, John, calling to him. Fritz let out a sigh. "Oh, Lord. Why is he here in the middle of the night? He should be sleeping in his own bed." John lived about one and a half miles away. Just as John was about to push the door open, thinking Fritz was too sound asleep to hear his knocking, Fritz opened it. Before Fritz stood his younger brother. His hair was covered in frost.

"Was tun Sie hier?"—What are you doing here?—

exclaimed Fritz in German, the men's native language. Things had not been very good between the brothers these past few weeks, and Fritz found himself short of temper when anything associated with his brother came up.

"I need a ride into New Glarus," John said. Fritz noticed that his brother appeared to be trembling from the frigid cold of the night air. He was also very agitated and tired; his eyes seemed lifeless.

As Fritz walked over to the fire and began to stoke the coals, attempting to get some heat into the room, he said, "Quiet down, not so loud, you will wake the children. Get over by the fire and warm up a little. Why do you need to go to New Glarus at this hour of the night?" Wisconsin winters were and still are vicious. Humble homes such as this one did not hold the heat very well, and then, only for a short time. They were not well insulated, as our homes are today.

John dropped the two cumbersome satchels he was carrying onto the floor. He also dropped two guns; both had been slung across his shoulder. "Did you walk here?" asked Fritz.

"Yes," John said, "I walked here. You know I do not have a horse; how else could I get here?"

John began to explain that he and Christen, his housemate, had accidentally shot a hog while hunting for rabbits, and the two knew they would be in trouble for it when the deed was discovered by the hog's owner. They decided to leave the area before anyone found out about the dead hog. John explained further that Christen had gone ahead to New Glarus and was waiting for him there.

Even though this story appeared to be fuzzy, Fritz relented and helped load the satchels into his wagon. He noticed that one was heavier than the other but did not say anything. After having a bite to eat, John asked for a photo of himself that he had left behind when he'd recently moved from his brother's home into his own place.

When the two men left the warmth of the house at about 5:30 a.m. for New Glarus, it was still dark and biting cold. As they first moved along, there was very little conversation between the two, and the only sounds were the plodding of the horse and the stirring of the wind in the trees that lined the road. John remained quiet until Fritz began to question his brother for more facts. He asked where he and Christen intended to go. John told him to Monroe, or perhaps—he mumbled and then paused, as though thinking—on to Chicago. After a long time, John mentioned he might go home to Switzerland. When asked about Christen's plans, he answered that he did not know what Christen would decide to do.

Fritz asked, "Do you have money?"

John replied, "Yes, I just got paid for the time I worked there." The brothers talked further about shooting the hog, but very little else.

Later, Fritz would wonder why he had not asked John what was in the heavy bag. He also thought of many more questions he should have asked at that time.

As Fritz was returning home after leaving John at the train station, his mind kept wandering back to the days when he and his younger brother were growing up in the Alps of Switzerland.

It seemed as though John had always been in trouble,

from the day he was born. The family noticed early on that there was something different about him; he was not quite like other children. As John grew up, he remained slow-minded, like a young child. His mind did not absorb things quickly, and he did not listen to his father at all. John was five years younger than Fritz, with their only sister, Elise, between them in age. Because Fritz was older, he was the one who had to keep John out of trouble during their youth.

John, always in trouble, caused his father, who could not or would not understand the problem, to take a horrible disliking to him. His father began to hate and despise John for the many naughty and strange things he did as a boy. Fritz was the one who covered up for his younger brother, especially when asked to do so by his mother because they both knew they must not let Papa know about another reason to dislike John. Eventually, their father threw John out of the family home, against the lament of his mother.

After the investigation that morning, Fritz was now sure John had lied to him about Christen having gone before him to the train. No one had seen either man since Friday, December 14. That was ten days ago. Where would John be now, he wondered? John had told Fritz he might go to Chicago. Why Chicago? Another puzzle.

Fritz had always been a reserved, healthy, and private person, and at this moment, he felt like crying. He felt particularly sad for his mother, so far away in Switzerland, and especially worried for his wife, Pauline. Both had been against John coming to America. Fritz was also anxious about the days to come and frightened for himself. This country was new to him, and the future he had looked forward to with such hopes, did not now seem so promising as he had once thought it would be. There was certainly much trouble to come for both himself and for his brother, John.

Fritz must have felt like gnashing his teeth to the bone, wishing he did not have John as a brother; he had enough problems without this horror. How could he continue to live in this neighborhood, or ever look his neighbors in the eye again? What would he tell his children?

Fritz must have also thought—people will think one brother is like the other. How can I possibly live through this?

Everyone on the jury would have returned to his home to tell what he had seen that morning. Many would have stopped at houses along the road home to relate the news, discussing the scene he had just left with his anxious and nosy neighbors. Word of mouth was the only way information moved from farm to farm during those days. Most of these people could not afford a daily paper, and if they received a weekly, it would not arrive at their home for many days. Neighbors needed to know the facts, and everyone was always eager to hear any news, especially about a scandal of any kind, most especially a murder.

Chapter Four
First Accounts

The first newspaper account of the horrible event came out two days later in the capital city of Madison, twenty miles away. On December 22, a banner headline in the *Wisconsin State Journal* delivered frightening news to its readers:

A HORRIBLE STORY NEAR MOUNT VERNON

The headline would cause even the busiest person to stop and read the story. It was two days before Christmas, and most people in the Madison area were thinking of getting groceries for the big day or perhaps planning a long ride to Grandma's house.

Below the headline, the reader's appetite for sensational news was fed by several paragraphs:

Yesterday as George Rea and his brother, William, were fishing on the West Branch of the Sugar River, they discovered a bag sunk in the river, and they fished it out. On investigation, they found it contained the head of a man. William Rea went to the nearest house, that of Mr. Narve Fyrge, who identified it as being the head of their cheesemaker, Wm Christ [sic], and on investigating the cheese factory, a horrible sight met their eyes....

...Wm Christ and Joseph Dahinden [sic], another cheesemaker were batching in the factory, and it is

supposed that this man was murdered, and in order to cover his crime, he started to burn the body, but it was too much of a job for him, so he tied the head in the sack and sunk it in the river and left.

The murderer was last seen on Thursday when Mr. Holland went to the factory where the boys worked and lived, but the fellow would not let him in and said everything was all right....

The deed reportedly occurred near Mount Vernon, the closest community to the cheese factory, which was about three miles away, and twenty miles southwest of Madison. Reading this story on a Tuesday morning in the local papers, the residents of the Madison area, shocked and horrified, were sent into a panic. A murder in Dane County! This was worse than anything they had ever heard of taking place in Wisconsin. Neither Dane nor Green County had seen a murder for many years. Accidental death, yes, but intentional and premeditated murder? No.

And the man who did this horrible thing was still out there, somewhere, possibly even in Madison. Twenty miles was not too far for someone to travel in several days. A murderer could be hiding in their neighborhood. Doors were quickly locked and kept locked for weeks. Everyone's ear was turned toward their front door, expecting a monster to break it down at any moment. The beast would have large hands and eyes that popped from his eye sockets. Of course, this would happen during the nighttime hours, so sleep was hard to come by.

Two days later, the *Wisconsin State Journal* carried a complete account of the event, filling in the details of the grisly story, which slowly began to unspool for the public. It was described in three long columns on page four, written in very small type. The headlines appeared as below:

HORRIBLE CRIME

Brutal Murder near Mount Vernon, Of this County
The Victim was Wm Christen, A Cheesemaker
Full Details of the Ghastly Tale

The tragedy, which has just come to light in Primrose, this county, proves even more horrible and brutal than reported in the State Journal on Saturday. The details show that no more cold-blooded, premeditated murder has ever been committed in the state of Wisconsin than the killing of William Christen, the Swiss cheesemaker, by his companion, John Kuhni...

The article goes on to describe the murderer. It also tells how John had recently been given naturalization papers by Mr. O'Connell, the clerk of court. It goes on to say that if John had skipped the country and because John was now a United States citizen (he actually was not a citizen, as he had only applied for the papers), it would be difficult to extradite him back to Wisconsin. John would have to be returned to Dane County for trial, and Judge Stewart would probably be the judge to try him, in what would be the county's first murder trial in many years.

Chapter Five
After Many Days

Before this time period, the township of Primrose had mostly been settled by Scandinavians. Only about twenty families of Swiss origin lived there in 1880, but the Swiss families from the New Glarus Colony in Green County were now gradually crowding out the Scandinavians in Dane County. It was mostly a farming area, and dairy was the chief industry. Primrose was a quiet, religious community, and never had a saloon until 1906. Among the area's first settlers was the La Follette family. Robert La Follette, who later became a United States senator and a Wisconsin governor, was born in the township of Primrose.

Until 1888, the Primrose area had never been touched by such a gruesome murder. Up and down the roads, neighbors expressed their disbelief that "this sort of thing" could happen in their quiet community, and in their backyard. Shop owners and office workers around the town square of Mount Vernon, the closest village, looked at each other and shook their heads. In the courthouse in Madison, lawyers and judges whispered and shook their heads. Everyone was in shock, and doors remained locked at night.

The account that ran in the *Madison Democrat* on Wednesday, December 24, 1888, made it clear that officials were now sure who the murderer was:

Search for the remains of William Christen, who was murdered at Primrose on 12 December and whose head was found in a sack in the river last Friday, continues, but without results.

It looks as though Christen was murdered while in bed, as the bedclothes were covered with blood. To cover the traces of his crime, Kuhni partially washed the blood-spattered walls, covered the bloodstains and clothes on the floor, and burned some of the bed clothing.

Chapter Six
Enter Sheriff Estes

The discovery of a corpse did not come to the attention of John Estes, sheriff of Dane County until a day and a half after the body parts were found in the creek. This would have been on Saturday, December 22. Only when a *Wisconsin State Journal* reporter approached the sheriff and asked for his comments was he made aware of the murder. There were few forms of communication between the countryside and the city at that time; news mostly traveled by word of mouth.

Once he heard the news, the sheriff left immediately for the township of Primrose, accompanied by his undersheriff, Vernon. The sheriff later related his frustration at not being notified of the "find" earlier. He said, "There was an inexcusable delay on the part of the proper authorities in informing me of the discovery of the brutal deed. Much time was lost because of this. However, once I arrived at the murder scene after a midnight ride to Mount Vernon, followed by a swift investigation, I immediately knew, without a doubt, who the murderer was. The deed was savage, and it did not take much investigation to figure out who did it.

"With the luck that somehow falls upon fiends for a time, our man now has a running start on us, and the scent is already cold behind him. But suddenly, our luck has changed, and we have discovered that he has left a broad trail for us, which we can easily follow."

Sheriff Estes continues:

"Within twenty-four hours from the time that the news of the murder reached us, we had located the man who did the murder. He was located onboard the steamship *Lord Gough*, somewhere on the high seas five days out from Philadelphia, bound for Basel, Switzerland. He would transfer at Queenstown, Ireland, to another ship, and again at Liverpool, England, before arriving at his final destination."

The article went on to tell what happened after Fritz left his brother at the New Glarus train station on Friday, December 14. John had boarded the train to Monticello and then traveled from there to Monroe, Wisconsin. There he purchased a train ticket from a steamship agent that would take him to Philadelphia. From here, he would sail on *Lord Gough* on December 19 to Switzerland, with a stop at Queenstown, Ireland, and also one at Liverpool, where he would change ships.

The newspapers around the state, especially the Dane County newspapers, continued to report daily the location of Kuhni. The "horrible crime," as the press was calling it, was the talk of the area, and then some. All kinds of rumors were flowing. Was Kuhni a serial killer? Would he come back and do more harm?

Whether Fritz Kuhni and his wife ever read the newspaper articles about John will never be known. Did Fritz receive a newspaper? Did he go out and purchase one? How much of this news did his parents back in Switzerland receive? Surely the news was known in their little Swiss village; the papers there probably published the story, in German, of course. This would have created a great deal of sadness, anger, and hopelessness for John's parents. Such a horror for them—how did they ever endure it? One can only imagine how devastated they must have felt to have a son do such a dastardly deed, and then to have it announced around the world.

&

On Monday, December 24,1888, the *Madison Democrat* headline read:

THE MURDERER LOCATED ON THE OCEAN

It was soon learned that John had insisted on taking the first available ship from the East Coast to Switzerland. That ship turned out to be a slow-moving ocean liner that took many days to arrive in Queenstown. He evidently thought getting away immediately would be his only way to escape from the authorities. Had he taken the time to wait in New York for a faster steamer, he would have landed before the message to arrest him arrived in England or Ireland.

There would have been much more to this story had he taken the faster line, as he could have reached Switzerland, where he was still a citizen, before being captured. Switzerland would not have allowed him to be extradited to America, and the trial would have had to be held there. Witnesses from Wisconsin would have had to be shipped there to give testimony.

On Monday, Estes traveled to Madison and consulted with Wisconsin's governor, Jeremiah Rusk. Rusk was a farmer, soldier, and politician who had commanded the 25th Wisconsin Infantry during the Civil War, and later served as Wisconsin's fifteenth governor, from 1882 to 1889.

Estes also met with District Attorney O'Connor. The governor telegraphed Secretary of State Thomas Bayard at Washington, D.C., with the information. Bayard later responded that the authorities at Queenstown, Ireland, would keep a watch out for Kuhni.

The team was fortunate to be able to telegraph information to faraway places. Prior to the telegraph, civilians would have relied on handwritten letters or messengers on foot to learn about family news. In emergency situations, families often would not learn about a crisis until several days after it happened.

The electric telegraph was invented in the early 1800s, allowing messages to travel quickly, even to faraway places. Samuel Morse, an inventor, one day received a note delivered to him by a messenger; he was horrified to read that his wife was seriously ill. By the time he arrived home to see her, she had died. This grave incident inspired Morse to develop a better and faster system of communication, along with a unique way of communication, which was available to the Dane County sheriff in 1888. With the stroke of a finger, Estes could send a message faster than sending his helper around the corner to another office with a sheet of paper. What a fantastic, modern world they now lived in.

The sheriff tells us in the Christmas morning edition of the *Madison Democrat*:

Extradition papers were immediately made out, and I then headed for Washington, D.C. I did not relish the idea of a lengthy trip to Europe, especially during this season of holidays and cold weather. It was a tough and hard decision for me to leave my family at Christmas, but I was ordered to go. I began to pack for the trip and quickly left my family behind to do my job; I had no choice.

By the time this article appeared in the paper, John Kuhni had been gone more than a week, and thoughts of what he had done and what could become of him if he were caught pulled John farther and farther from the crime scene, and closer to his former home, a more familiar and safer place. He was attempting to return to his roots, to his parents, and possibly to friends, if he had any.

He was almost home, back to his beautiful mountains, back to his mother, who understood him. He would definitely have been bewildered and confused about his memories of the crime, and undoubtedly frightened about his future.

Why he thought his home country or his family would save him, we will never know.

Chapter Seven
John's Heritage

The Kuehni family originally came from Langnau in the Emmental Valley, Canton (County) of Bern, in the heart of Switzerland, about fifteen miles east of Bern. Langnau means "in the valley."

Set in a forest, Langnau im Emmental is a beautiful and very wealthy village with lots of hills surrounding it. It was built on higher ground along one of the streams flowing into the Emme River. Watered by the Alps, it is the most fertile area in Switzerland. The region is mostly devoted to farming, particularly dairy farming.

The name Kühni is found as far back as records exist for the area. The original spelling of the name Kuehni deletes the "e" and places an umlaut over the letter "u."

Members of the Kühni family were free farmers, herdsmen, tradesmen, soldiers, or mercenaries, all of a small class of free landholders of intermediate status. They were not members of the local aristocracy, nor of the more significant number of indentured peasants and serfs.

❦

Fritz (Fredrick) Kuhni came to America in 1883, having followed some of his fellow countrymen to the area of New Glarus, Wisconsin. There had been few jobs available in Switzerland to offer much of a future for a young man with a new wife; the future there appeared dim. Southern Wisconsin, the area where many other Swiss immigrants had settled before him, resembled the terrain of the foothills of the Alps, where he had grown up. Fritz had saved his money and followed his dreams to America, a poor immigrant hoping to improve conditions for his family.

Fritz was the first of the Kuhni family to emigrate to America, but he would be followed by most of his generation, and the following generation, of his family. Fritz and his wife first settled in Green County near New Glarus; their first son was born there shortly after they arrived. Most of the men in his family were cheesemakers, and this Swiss family chose this area not only because of the strong Swiss heritage that had settled there before them but also because of the strong support of cheesemaking. Some of his neighbors were from the same area of Switzerland he had come from; they spoke the same language, making him feel very welcome.

The Kuhni family attempted to retain their native language, livelihoods, food, and customs, the reasons they chose to settle with others who had come from the same area in Switzerland. They worshipped in churches that observed the same age-old rites and customs they were accustomed to in the old country.

Families living on farms in the country traveled into the nearby villages for essential services, such as blacksmithing, harness making, and general stores for flour, etc.

History tells us that during the early 1900s, Green County was one of the wealthiest counties in Wisconsin. This was mostly due to the many dairy farms found there and the little colony of Swiss people who knew how to make good use of each cow.

However, they soon discovered that the land was poorly adapted to farming, as the area was hilly, with sandy soil filled with stones and rocks. Many of the Swiss settlers decided to return to what their ancestors were trained to do, and that was to make cheese. They purchased cows from the East Coast and began to process cheese. By 1916, there were 153 cheese factories and three creameries in the county.

New Glarus, Green County, Wisconsin, was and still is one of the largest Swiss settlements in the United States. Until 1850, it was known as the Swiss Colony. It is located about sixteen miles north of Monroe and about twenty-five miles south of Madison, the state capital.

New Glarus was founded in 1845 by impoverished citizens of Glarus, Switzerland. At that time, much of Europe was in the grips of severe depression, food was in short supply, and jobs were equally scarce. In response to this crisis, the Swiss government formed the Swiss Emigration Society. The society offered passage to America for anyone who wanted to leave Switzerland. On April 16, 1845, a ship left for the United States with 193 Glarus subjects. Four months later, on August 16, these pioneers arrived in Wisconsin, in the area that would become New Glarus.

The founding of this community might be one of the finest examples of the best of socialism. Each settler received twenty acres of land apportioned by a lottery; the property could not be exchanged. The colonists worked together and looked out for the welfare of all, providing schooling, food, shelter, and health care. The oxen teams needed to work the land were communally owned, as was most of the machinery.

Any Swiss immigrant would feel at home there, as it resembled the country they had left behind. The countryside was soon speckled with cows wearing bells, just as they did in Switzerland, and the new settlers found the sound soothing to their ears. The nearby forests provided plenty of wood for their stoves in the winter and lumber for constructing their buildings.

As soon as those first families were settled, they ordered enough cattle from Ohio to allow one for each family, along with a shared bull for all.

Even though the early Swiss families had to undergo many changes and hardships after settling in Green County, they always kept up their homeland spirit and passed it on to their children. For many years the people spoke the Glarner-German language mixed with some English and eventually gave in to speaking English only.

They experienced no class oppression compared to their old country and found that here in Wisconsin, they could talk to anyone without having to remove their headgear and bow. The simple, hardworking farmer and the highest officials received the same respect.

The Swiss-American woman was pleasantly surprised to learn she could enjoy much greater freedom and rights than she had in Switzerland. For example, here in Wisconsin, the man of the family did not have the right to sell his home without the consent of his wife. Women quickly took over some of the reins of the family and soon became members of school boards and other community offices, in addition to doing most of the household business. Women dressed simply, but always in spotlessly clean clothing. Men, whether dressed in shabby or new clothing, were not humiliated.

Churches did not receive any support from the government. In the early days, no birth, marriage, and death records were kept, causing many problems later.

Food was simple and much the same as they were used to in Switzerland. The most popular drink among the Swiss settlers was beer, the same as the German immigrants who had settled nearby. In 1890, beer could be purchased at the local brewery for $1 per gallon. In saloons, a beer cost five cents per glass, as did one cigar.

Today, New Glarus, named after the Swiss canton of Glarus, and known as "America's Little Switzerland," retains its old-world charm. A visit to the Swiss Historical Village makes one feel like they're in Switzerland, with buildings characteristic of the Alps and Swiss flags flying alongside American flags.

Three years after arriving in Wisconsin in 1883, Fritz and his family moved from Green County to Dane County, a few miles north, near the township of Primrose. By about 1886, he was working as a cheesemaker in Section 16, in Primrose. I believe he was living in the apartment of the cheese factory where he worked.

One day, Fritz received a letter from his sister in Switzerland saying that his wayward brother, John, age 26, would be joining him in the new world; John was already on his way to America. Fritz and his wife were not happy about this news. They had received an earlier letter from Fritz's sister telling him that John had spent several years in prison. The family later learned he had spent from January 30, 1884, to April 14, 1887, in a Swiss prison for breaking and entering.[3]

It would have been impossible for John to find work near his home after his prison sentence, and he could not go home, as his father had utterly abandoned him. The family lived near a small village in a remote part of Switzerland where everyone knew what everyone else was doing, and had done, for their entire life. The family evidently decided John should go to America. His family hoped this history would not come to light in the United States. (They may also have had some help in making this decision and paying for the trip from the local police department or the Swiss government.)

Appalled, Fritz and his wife, Pauline, did not want John to join their small household. Yet, Fritz could not say no to his parents, even though he knew John would be a handful. Besides, his brother was already on the way to America—how could he send him back? There was no money to pay for such a trip. They would, somehow, have to make this work.

John made the trip to the United States alone, as far as I know, probably leaving from the port of Le Havre in France. He was allowed to enter the country because he had a brother here to sign for him. Because Ellis Island was not open for business until 1892, arrivals were processed at a landing depot in New York City's Battery Park known at the time as Castle Garden. As they arrived, the Swiss

---

[3] Bern Archives

men and women, whether they spoke German, French, or Italian, were assisted by a clerk who could speak their language or dialect. Their names and particulars would have been recorded and checked against the ship's passenger list before they were helped on their way. A clerk probably helped John with directions to a train or other transportation, as he would have had trouble understanding the ways of this new country. Remember, he was not very bright, and had never been away from the foothills of the Alps, had never lived in a large city.

He made his way to Dane County, Wisconsin, where his brother lived, about June of 1887, and began working as a cheesemaker. Cheesemaking was big business in that part of Wisconsin at the time, and trained cheesemakers were needed. John, like his brother, had grown up working in cheese factories, and knew how to do the basic jobs necessary in that field; even with limited education, he could work as an assistant.

At first, things were all right with an additional person in their household, but eventually, Fritz had to ask John to leave his home when his violent and obnoxious disposition became too much for Pauline. He found John a job as a cheesemaker in another local factory about one and a half miles away. John would be working with another Swiss immigrant, William Christen, who had emigrated from the same area the Kuhni brothers had come from. We do not know if they knew each other before leaving Switzerland, but if not, they had much in common and would have been naturally drawn to each other.

Life had been hard in Switzerland, but evidently, things were not so great here, either, because we find John living in terrible poverty in December of 1888. He was living with Christen in a cheese factory, known as the Holland Factory, located between the houses of A. S. Holland and John Gruening. Holland and Gruening were co-owners of the factory building. The cheese factory was located in Section 16 in the township of Primrose, three miles south and west of the town of Mount Vernon. The Holland family owned 282 acres, having settled in the area before 1873. They farmed the land around their home, as did their neighbors, and the milk they produced was taken to the factory for processing into cheese.

When Wisconsin was first settled, the only money-making crop was wheat. Before the 1850s, cheesemaking in Wisconsin was done in the rural homes of families who had brought their recipes from Europe. It was always done by the women in the family. Making cheese was not to be done by men; it was considered demeaning. To the wheat farmer, caring for cows and making cheese was beneath his dignity; he was a man of the soil. Women did all the milking and caring for the cows, as well as making the cheese and butter.

For years in the United States, cheesemaking was considered a home craft, like canning vegetables. The churning process was casual and usually unsanitary, and families made no effort to control what their cows ate. As a result, many noxious and unwholesome odors, from dirty laundry to wild onions and garlic, found their way into the butter and cheese. Shopkeepers did no inspecting, and butter and cheese were lumped into barrels with no quality control.

However, as wheat was planted year after year in the same fields, the crop began to decrease, even in the fertile Wisconsin soil. The weather was also a problem; each year, there was either too much rain or too little.

Slowly, economics forced farmers to change from wheat crops to dairy cows. It was either give up farming completely or change over to cows. The old wheat fields began to be sowed with clover and grass, and cows began to graze in those former wheat fields, and barns to house the cattle sprang up all over. Some hoped to return to wheat farming someday, but it did not happen, causing some settlers to give up and leave for the "far west."

The men in the Kuhni family, like Wisconsin's other Swiss immigrants, were acquainted with making cheese in the Alps of Switzerland. They knew how to make good Swiss and Limburger cheeses, as they enjoyed the taste of those. It was their main source of protein. The Swiss families relocating to Wisconsin would have made Swiss cheese, first in their kitchens, and then gradually moving the stinky task to a barn or other outbuilding.

Cheesemaking was more profitable than making butter because it used the whole milk and required less refrigeration. But because cheese required more knowledge and skill than butter, it was practiced by only a handful of Wisconsin farmers.

Cheesemaking is both a skill and an art, and the immigrants brought this knowledge with them from Switzerland, handed down in each family for generations. A young man in the old country who chose to go into cheesemaking would have had to apprentice before he was qualified to be a cheesemaker.

In southern Wisconsin, an experienced cheesemaker would have found a different type of feed for his cattle, a warmer climate, and other causes to adjust his techniques, but the adjustments were easily made.

❧

Wisconsin's first commercial cheese factory came on the scene in 1864 moving cheesemaking out of the kitchens of private homes. Soon, more cheese factories rose on the horizon, purchasing milk from the area farmers.

At first, the Swiss farmers did not like the idea of selling their milk to cheese factories. They were very satisfied making cheese at home from their own milk. They thought that the peculiar way of making Swiss cheese they had learned in Switzerland could not be duplicated in a large-scale production system.

There were many reasons the farmer did not like to haul his milk to a factory. One was that the cheesemaker had to have all of the day's milk in the vat at the same time to begin making the cheese. This meant the farmer had to be on time every day, and they were not used to being on time or being told what to do. The factories also demanded cleanliness, which the farmers had a tendency to ignore.

Most farmers cut and stored only enough hay to keep their animals alive during the winter months, and made no effort to milk their cows after October. They believed that the winter "rest" increased output during the summer milking season. When the cheese factory closed for the winter months, as they did in the early years of cheesemaking, those farmers who milked their cows year-round had to make their own cheese and butter, or dry up their cows.

However, once the farmers discovered that hauling milk to a cheese factory was a money-making project, they began selling their milk to the new cheese factories. They also discovered that the cheese made in the factories was of much better and more uniform quality than the cheese they made in their home kitchens.

The top local cheesemakers began to build and operate more and more factories. A skilled cheesemaker might supervise the production of cheese in as many as twenty factories. Each owner would hire other cheesemakers to operate the various facilities, purchase milk from farmers, and provide the necessary supplies. Each factory specialized in one kind of cheese; there were four hundred varieties made in the area at the time. Swiss and Limburger became the most popular cheeses made by the native Swiss people.

By 1885, Green County had 104 cheese factories. In 1890, there were one thousand cheese factories throughout the state of Wisconsin.

Swiss cheese was made in huge copper kettles that could hold up to two thousand gallons of milk. The milk was heated to 120 degrees over a wood fire. After enzymes from a calf's stomach were added to the warmed milk, the milk turned into about three hundred pounds of curd. The cheesemaker skillfully placed a sheet of cheesecloth around the curd, which was then carried on a pulley system across the room and forced into a wooden press in the shape of a wheel. This wheel reduced the curd to about two hundred pounds of cheese.

Swiss cheese was first taxed in Europe by the piece, not by weight, which is why cheese was made in large wheels.

This tradition continued for years.

Swiss cheese was considered to improve as it aged. In Switzerland, it was a custom in some families to make a cheese wheel on the day a child was born. The cheese would be kept and served on the child's birthdays and wedding day. Sometimes it was held as long as eighty years and served at their funeral.

A few other interesting facts about cheese:

- Swiss cheese has eyes, some as large as a quarter. No, Swiss cheese holes are not the result of mice.
- Blind cheese is cheese without eyes!
- A Swiss harp is used to cut the cheese curd.
- Cheddar and Swiss cheeses ripen from the inside out, while brick and Limburger ripen from the outside in.

Along with Swiss and Swiss brie, Limburger cheese became very popular in Wisconsin and was made in smaller portions than the Swiss style. The cheese was aged in a basement, called a cellar, where it slowly acquired a yellow mold that every other day had to be "smeared" to rub the whiskers off by hand. I remember my aunt Bert talking about this distasteful job that was handed to her as she was growing up. She often related how the house she lived in was old and primitive, and that she had to endure the odor of this horrible job. She said the house always smelled of Limburger cheese.

It was customary in this part of the state for the cheesemaker or the owner to live at the factory, and if the factory-made Limburger cheese, the smell was ever-present throughout the building. The smell develops late in the process of aging, and if you ate or sold Limburger before it became too old, the smell was not bad at all. After three weeks, the Limburger was packaged in parchment and tin foil and aged for three more weeks. That is when the smell would really appear!

At first, the Limburger cheese, popular with the local Swiss and the Germans to the east, would be hauled by wagon to the railroad station to be shipped to the Milwaukee area. The smell of this cheese in the station caused the local children to hold their noses in disgust.

William Christen, employed as a cheesemaker at the Holland Cheese Factory, completed his cheesemaking for the season on November 27. Christen had come from the area of Leimisyl, Switzerland, only a mile or so from where John and his brother, Fritz, had grown up. They probably went to school together. John had been an assistant to Christen at the Holland factory for about two months.

Christen was already living at the factory when John moved there after being "turned away" from his brother's home. Fritz lived one and a half miles east of the factory at another factory called the Peterson Cheese Factory, which later became known as the Standard Cheese Factory, in Section 15.

John easily made friends with Christen because they were fellow countrymen and spoke the same language. They seemed to be compatible. Each loved whiskey, according to some locals. "John was a loafer and hanger-on about the place, worthless and whiskey-loving," according to one person.

"William Christen was not far behind John in this last respect," according to another, "although he seemed to be an industrious fellow." [4]

During the long winter months, cheesemakers would keep themselves busy by repairing items and making wooden cheese boxes to use for shipping the cheese the following year. This was also a time to read, pursue hobbies, and take life easy. When dairy calves were born in the spring, the milk would again "come in" to the mother. Cows were milked, and once again, the milk was available for hauling to the factories, where cheesemaking began again.

Living together, the men prepared their own meals and hunted for their meat. John had recently purchased a gun with some of his earnings. There was plenty of small game around, and the two men did a lot of hunting for squirrels and rabbits. A branch of the Sugar River ran past the factory, which provided fish for meals. Even though it was a very shallow stream, there was one deep hole a few yards from the factory that always held a good supply of fish.

---

[4] Unknown neighbor

Chapter Eight
The Long Chase

After much preparation and tears when parting with his family, Sheriff Estes, traveling by train, left Madison, Wisconsin, for Washington, D.C., on Christmas morning. This was the beginning of his long chase after the fugitive Kuhni.

An interview between Estes and a reporter from the *Wisconsin State Journal* on February 18, 1889 reads:

On the way to Washington, I read over the somewhat voluminous documents containing the evidence. Each time that I read over them, my faith in them was weakened. I realized that the testimony elicited at the coroner's request was purely circumstantial and not very strong at that.

Also, in the hurried preparations of papers, a confusion of names had arisen. In the proceedings at the inquest, the murderer was spoken of as Hans Kuhni, while throughout the balance of the papers, his name appeared as John Kuhni. John Kuhni was the name under which he sailed for Europe.

The case would be considered very strong in Dane County, Wisconsin, where the air was rife with rumor and suspicion, but I feared that it would lose much of its intensity when subjected to the cooling influences of crossing the ocean.

When arriving in Washington, D.C., I immediately contacted Wisconsin Representative, Robert La Follette, who was in the city that day. We, together, visited the state department and had a lengthy conversation with Third Assistant Secretary, Moore, who had charge of matters pertaining to extradition.

I communicated my suspicions about not having enough evidence or personal identification of Kuhni to our good friend, La Follette. He accompanied me to the department of state, and as a result, a telegram was sent to Wisconsin asking additional depositions to be forwarded immediately.

Representative La Follette took an active interest in myself and this case. Not only did the murder occur in the township where he was living, but he was assisting in preparing the new United States Agent, myself, in being able to "fully act for our country" after reaching England. While in Washington, D.C., our Wisconsin Representative was my guide and special bodyguard, giving me every assistance possible in his friendly and genial way. I was entertained very hospitably by both he and his admirable wife.[5]

Sheriff Estes was then provided with a most important and proper warrant, signed by President Cleveland. All the necessary papers were transferred to the American legation in London. Copies were sent to ensure the detention of Kuhni on his landing in England. Estes was formally appointed a United States marshal and invested with the power to act for the government of the United States. He was then known as Captain Estes.

---

[5] *Madison Democrat*, 18 Feb. 1889

❧

United States marshals are called upon to uphold the government's interests and policies in a wide variety of circumstances. From 1796 to 1896, marshals were paid on a fee system, collecting a set amount for a particular task. These marshals answered only to the president and were appointed or dismissed only by the president, until 1861, when Congress assigned full supervision of marshals to the attorney general. In 1863, local district judges were granted authority to appoint, supervise, and dismiss marshals.

Once appointed, the federal government seldom gave marshals any type of guidance; they were on their own. No one explained what was expected of them. Each marshal was appointed because it was believed he had enough sense to know what to do. He was not required to wear a uniform and did not receive a badge stating his commission. If the appointed marshal wanted to wear a badge, he did so at his own expense. He received only a large, fancily worded commission signed by the president. [6]

Estes delayed his overseas trip in order to procure a photo of Kuhni, who had gathered the only known photo of himself from his brother's house. A copy was ordered from a photographer in Madison who was believed to have

---

[6] Frederick S. Calhoun, *The Lawmen: United States Marshals and Their Deputies, 1789-1989*

taken that photo.

Estes was told that a full and detailed description of Kuhni would be required when he reached England. He telegraphed Wisconsin Governor Rusk and asked to have this material cabled to Queenstown, Liverpool, and Scotland Yard, taking every precaution to secure Kuhni before he could leave British soil.

Estes was concerned that if John should reach Switzerland, his native land, he couldn't be brought back to Wisconsin, owing to the nature of that country's extradition laws. This would mean John would face trial there, and any witnesses would have to be sent overseas to testify, a very expensive endeavor.

Back in Dane County, work continued on the "horrible Primrose crime," as everyone was calling it. It was still the talk of the town. The sheriff's department was busy rounding up witnesses for John's anticipated Wisconsin trial and entering them into the court system. A deputy under Sheriff Vernon delivered subpoenas to the townships of Blue Mound, Springdale, and Primrose in Dane County, and to the towns of New Glarus and Monroe in Green County. Witnesses contacted at this time were Rudy Regetz, John Anderson, A. S. Holland, Jacob Bruni, Fred Kuhni, William and George Ray, Mathias Mathiasen, N. Byrge, P. A. Sangesand, and J. Tschudy.

On December 26, newspapers reassured the public that John would be returned to Wisconsin shortly, as the proper authorities in Queenstown had promised to detain him until Sheriff Estes arrived there. However, it would probably be at least three weeks before he could be returned to Wisconsin. Again on December 27, an article assured readers that the police at Liverpool, Queenstown, and Scotland Yard in London were all on the alert for the murderer.

⋙

On December 28, the *Madison Democrat* reported:

From a Washington D.C. dispatch, Kuhni will arrive in Queenstown today or tomorrow, and he will be secured upon landing... Before leaving the country, Sheriff Estes was provided with the proper warrant pertaining to extradition....

The newspaper's issue of the twenty-ninth announced that a telegram had been received from the sheriff stating, that he would board a fast Cunarder for England armed with the proper papers to secure the fugitive. It was learned at Philadelphia that Kuhni had attempted to change his name, but that this had not been permitted, as he was already docketed on *Lord Gough* under his real name.

Launched in November 1878, *Lord Gough* was chartered to the American Steamship Line and made her maiden voyage from Liverpool to Philadelphia in April 1879. In 1888 she was bought by the Lord Gough Steamship Co. (American Line) but continued to sail under the British flag.

It was also learned that John had never had a photo taken of himself in Madison, as was previously thought.

The known photo had been taken in Switzerland before he left the country. Someone had falsely reported that John had his photo taken the week before the tragedy.

It was announced that three telegrams had been sent by officials in Washington, one each to Queenstown, Liverpool, and Scotland Yard. It was only sixty minutes from the time they were sent that answers were received in the Madison office confirming their receipt. It was noted that this was a considerably shorter time than it sometimes took a messenger boy to serve a telegram one block away from an office in Washington, D.C.

In Madison, anxiety about the murder began to fade with the knowledge that Kuhni was an ocean away. Normal activities commenced, as shown by an announcement in the Wisconsin *State Journal* soliciting any lady who desired to hold an "open house" for New Year's Day to contact the paper for publication. Life went on, and Christmas and New Year celebrations continued as always.

Chapter Nine
Estes Trip to Europe

Immediately below the article referenced above, on page two of the *Madison Democrat*, was an accompanying piece. The headline read:

AFTER THE MURDERER

A dispatch from Washington says:

It is supposed that Kuhni will arrive in Queenstown today or tomorrow, and every precaution is being taken to secure him.

The following is an account of Estes's trip to Queenstown, written in my words and based on Estes's report found in the *Wisconsin State Journal* on February 18, 1889, after he returned to the United States.

The ship backed out of her slip late in the afternoon. There were two tugboats assisting the monster steamer in turning her prow seaward, and the ship soon followed the circuitous channel of New York harbor down past the Statue of Liberty and Sandy Hook and then out to sea.

A great crowd had gathered to witness the boat's departure, and he stood on the hurricane near the gangplank and witnessed the farewells of friends to others departing the country.

He overheard one old lady remark, as she bid a tearful adieu to a friend, "I will meet you soon upon the other shore." Which shore would that possibly be, he wondered?

Estes related how he watched the departure of the ship with great interest, as this was his first trip on the water, and he was very anxious about doing everything correctly. He noted that the duties of the crew and officers were performed with military precision. This kept him in contemplation until he considered the fact that he was backed up by old Dane County and the U.S. government. What could go wrong when he had the necessary papers in his pocket signed by the President of the United States, the highest official in the world? He related how he was able to then slowly relax and continue the long trip with less fear of causing problems or other incidents to occur.

Estes certainly could relax, as the United States government had placed him on the SS *Servia*, the first "modern" ocean liner, a transatlantic passenger and mail steamer of revolutionary design, launched in 1881. She was the first large ocean liner to be built of steel instead of iron, and the first Cunard ship to have electric lighting.

Servia was the first liner to specialize in passenger transportation and was considered to be the first liner of what became known as the "Express Transatlantic Service."

Servia had public rooms of an unprecedented scale and luxury, including a first-class smoking room, a luxuriously fitted ladies' drawing-room, and a music room. The entrance and grand staircase, paneled in polished maple and ash, were the largest that had ever appeared on a liner. The staircase led down to a landing on the main deck, which featured a library. Twenty-four first-class staterooms were situated aft of this landing, while the first-class dining salon was situated forward. The dining salon could seat 220 of *Servia*'s 480 first-class passengers at five long tables and was richly decorated with carved panels and carpets.

Yes, I think Estes was very pleased with his ride to Europe as he had not been raised in any sort of luxury of any kind.

His story continues in my words:

The first three days out at sea were very pleasant but at the end of that time a storm of considerable magnitude set in which caused the ship to rock and roll, heave and pitch, causing the Dane County sheriff, or rather the newly appointed United States Agent, some degree of sea-sickness. The ship was "heaving," and that is just what he felt like doing — heaving.

For the next three days, the sea, his head and his stomach were in a tempestuous and turbulent condition. He decided that such a thing as a pleasant ocean voyage was a delusion and a snare. He found that he felt like shooting the first man he heard quoting the verse, "A Life on the Ocean Wave."

On the seventh day of the voyage, it was announced that Ireland would be reached about 9 p.m. that evening. As that hour approached, the passengers were anxiously peering through the darkness for the coast light. For four days, the captain had not been able to take an observation, due to fog, but had made his calculations by the dead reckoning. The passengers were told that the Irish coast was bold and rocky and that shipwrecks were no uncommon thing. The dapper Captain, under the name of Horatio McKay, had been parading around the *"Servia"* in his glittering uniform and acting like he knew what he was doing. Everyone was concerned and wondered if, with all the difficulties and dangers ahead, the Captain could rise to the challenge and get them safely landed.

They did not have long to wait as suddenly, through the pitch-darkness, they caught a gleam of light, and knew that all was well. All onboard decided that Captain McKay was one of the skillful navigators for which the Cunarders were famed.

They reached Queenstown, Ireland, on 7 January, and Estes remained there just long enough to learn that Kuhni had indeed been arrested after the ship was boarded by Irish officers and had been sent on to London. As quick as steam would carry him, he was in Liverpool, and then a short and interesting train ride to the world's metropolis, London.

Sergeant Froest, the detective who had made the arrest, met him at the depot. He told Estes that upon the arrival of Lord Gough at Queenstown, he had found Kuhni among the steerage passengers.

He related to Estes how the detective, with handcuffs in his hand, had advanced toward John ready to shackle him, John quickly backed away, saying, "I am not a bad man, and those things (he pointed at the handcuffs) say I am a bad man."

The detective then called two brawny Irish detectives to his assistance, and the man was soon overpowered and quickly placed in irons. Kuhni was a strong man, and he fought desperately, the Sergeant later related.[7]

John had been captured on the steamer, *Lord Gough*, by the Queenstown authorities. When first questioned by authorities, he stated that he knew nothing of the crime, putting a bold face on the matter. Officers on board the vessel during the trip over the Atlantic reported that John had acted strangely throughout the journey. No details on precisely what "strange" meant.

He was remanded to wait for the arrival of Sheriff Estes with the necessary papers before anything would further happen.

Meanwhile, the officers at Liverpool, England, were also anxiously watching for Kuhni, in case the Queenstown police had missed him. They soon received a dispatch from Queenstown announcing his arrest. They could now forget about this fugitive and go on with other problems.

The *Milwaukee Journal* of Monday, December 31, 1888, carried a headline that read:

NOT A MURDERER
Hans Kuhni Protests His Innocence
Declaring his Arrest an Unmerited Disgrace

Followed by:

---

7 *Madison Democrat*, 18 Feb. 1889

The prisoner, Kuhni, in Queenstown, is claiming that he knew nothing of the murder of which he was charged. He said that he did not object to returning to Wisconsin, but he thought his arrest was an unmerited disgrace and went on to say that he was not fleeing his country, but openly returning to his country where his family lived. He told how he had become tired of Wisconsin and wished to return to his family and home.

The officers of the ship were interviewed and told that John had acted strangely during the cruise. His luggage was examined and itemized. Listed was two silver watches, three chains, a flannel shirt saturated with blood, a pair of canvas trousers with bloodstains on them, a pair of boots stained with something not yet analyzed, a large clasp knife smeared with blood, a gun which had been dismantled, some cartridges and a certificate of naturalization for the State of Wisconsin.

(It was probably an application for papers, not the final forms.)

On December 31, a cable from Queenstown arrived in Wisconsin, saying that John Kuhni was arrested on the steamer *Lord Gough* when she reached Queenstown from Philadelphia. On January 2, they received another cable about the arraignment to be held on January 4 in London.[8]

He was held in prison in Queenstown, Ireland until the

---

[8] *Milwaukee Journal,* 31 December, 1889

production of proof sufficient to warrant his arrest arrived along with ex-Sheriff Estes, who would have the necessary papers for his extradition.[9]

&

Back home in Wisconsin, it was frigid cold, but then Wisconsin is always cold in January. The readers of newspapers in Madison and Dane County were relieved to know that this "horrible creature" had been captured, was being held in custody, and could no longer hurt anyone.

It was now the year 1889, the year the Eiffel Tower opened in Paris. Adolph Hitler was born in Austria in April of that year, and in May, the horrific Johnstown, Pennsylvania, flood occurred, killing at least 2,200 people. In the latter part of 1889, North and South Dakota, followed by Montana and Washington, were admitted to the United States as states. It was also the year Benjamin Harrison took office as the U.S. president.

Harrison was an American politician and lawyer who served as the twenty-third president of the United States from 1889 to 1893. He was a grandson of the ninth president, William Henry Harrison, creating the only grandfather-grandson duo to have held the office. An American military officer and politician, William Henry Harrison served in 1841. He died of typhoid fever thirty-one days into his term, thereby serving the shortest tenure in United States presidential history.

---

[9] *Wisconsin State Joural,* 2 January, 1889

Chapter Ten
Queenstown to London

An Associated Press dispatch from London read:

First Arraignment in Queenstown
Monday, January 1, 1889

Kuhni, the man who was arrested at Queenstown on the charge of being a fugitive murderer from Wisconsin, was taken from there to London and arraigned in the Bow Street Police Court today. He was remanded for a further hearing while waiting for the arrival of Sheriff Estes.

Queenstown, later known as Cobh (pronounced Cove), is on the southern coast of County Cork, Ireland. John would have been placed on another steamship to cross the sea between Ireland and Liverpool, England, and then taken on a short train ride to London.

∾

Back home in Wisconsin, the *Wisconsin State Journal* on January 5, 1889, reported that the body of William Christen had not yet been discovered, and it was very probable that it might never be found unless Kuhni returned to southern Wisconsin and disclosed its whereabouts. John was the only person alive who knew where he buried the remains, and the area is covered with countless acres of woodland.

A thorough search was made of the factory, barns, wells, creeks, fields, and nearby woods by willing volunteers. It was possible Kuhni had carried off part of the body in one of his satchels, as it had been reported that blood had been seen leaking from his bag. Some authorities presumed that he could have removed the body parts from his satchel after departing Monticello and hidden them somewhere local. One newspaper article said that it was believed that the body was buried in a swampy area farther upstream from where the head was found.

John's brother, Fritz, reported that he had noticed that one of John's bags was very heavy. Another report of a satchel had been found along the railroad by section hands near Monroe was later declared to be false, according to Sheriff Struthers of Monroe. The article also reported that it had been discovered Kuhni had been in Madison the previous fall and had his photo taken there.

Lots of speculation.

More and more facts were beginning to surface, and the newspaper reporters continued with their wild stories.

It was now January of another year and the occupants of the capital of Madison were consumed with planning the inaugural ceremonies for the new governor, William Hoard, who was replacing the previous governor, Jeremiah Rusk. Hoard and his family arrived by special train from Fort Atkinson for a full day of ceremonies. The "horrible murder" would be set aside and forgotten for a while.

Widely considered the father of the Wisconsin dairy industry, William Dempster Hoard (1836-1918) played a prominent role in the development of the School of Agriculture at the University of Wisconsin and began *Hoard's Dairyman*, which is still published to this day. By the 1880s, his reputation had spread beyond Wisconsin, resulting in his producing a new weekly publication, *Hoard's Dairyman*, the first national dairy magazine in the country. He was in great demand as a speaker throughout the state and he easily won the next election as the "Cow Candidate." Hoard's election was generally considered the start of Wisconsin's progressive political tradition. He served as governor from 1889 to 1891.

An article in the *Madison Democrat* of January 8, 1889, reads:

Governor Hoard announces that a cablegram arrived this morning from Agent Estes, announcing his safe arrival in London, where he is stationed at the Cordon Hotel on the Strand. He says all looks well for the extradition of Kuhni, the murderer of Christen, the Swiss cheesemaker in Primrose of Dane County.

Chapter Eleven
The Examination—London

However, when Agent Estes arrived in London on January 7, 1889, everything was not so well as he had been told. He was informed that it would be impossible to see the prisoner until Kuhni was brought into the court for examination, which would not be for three more days. Estes quickly learned that the rules and regulations governing London prisons were different from those in the United States and that he had no choice except to wait.

The examination was held four days later at the Bow Street Police Court on January 11 and presided over by Sir James Ingham. This was the first time Agent Estes had seen the prisoner.

On Feb 18, 1889, the *Madison Democrat* provided a detailed interview with Estes about the London Court Proceedings. Below is a summation of such:

A large and curious crowd had assembled to witness the proceedings, which was very common at the time. People seemed to have time to spend in court watching the actions of the court.

Kuhni was brought in and placed in the prisoner's dock, a cage set above the main floor, so everyone could easily see him.

The Swiss Consul, located in London, was also in the courtroom every time that Kuhni was arraigned from then on. John's London attorney, Mr. Arthur Newton, was also present. Mr. Newton translated the language used by John to the court.

Detective Froest provided the court with evidence regarding specific articles found among the prisoner's effects, among other things exhibiting a bloody shirt, overalls, and a knife. The conclusion by Estes was that not only had Kuhni apparently coolly murdered and robbed his friend and benefactor, and then mutilated his body, but had, with reckless carelessness carried the evidence of his guilt with him 4,000 miles away from the scene of the tragedy.

Indeed, everyone there that day wondered why the man would carry this damming evidence with him, especially across an ocean; he surely could not be very intelligent!

Agent Estes was then called to the stand to testify to the genuineness of the various signatures and seals attached to the extradition documents.

As the examination continued, it was obvious that every listener there that day was entirely convinced of the prisoner's guilt but also was much shocked at the coolness and indifference, which he showed. There was one moment that John became very agitated when the blood-stained garments were shown, but he soon composed himself. From that time on, he remained, throughout the examination, apparently as unconcerned as if he had nothing to do with what he was accused of.

The volunteer counsel that had been appointed for John began to attack the evidence and raised the question of the prisoner's identity. He noted that in the application for extradition, two different first names had been used, Hans and John. He told the court that in the coroner's inquest, the man was recorded as John Kuhni. "My client is John Kuhni, "he replied. "Since my client is charged with such an atrocious crime, for which he will pay the extreme penalty of the law, testimony more positive than, that which has been offered, should be presented to secure his extradition."

Agent Estes again took the stand. He explained that one of the names was that under which he sailed and the other one by which the prisoner was most commonly known as in the neighborhood in which he lived. He took from his pocket the original description of the prisoner as he had obtained from John's brother, Fritz. Here he had noted that the name was Hans or John Kuhni and that he used both names to identify himself.

He read the description of John to the court, and all agreed that it fitted him exactly. The magistrate then asked Estes if he knew the prisoner personally. Estes answered that he had never met John before this time and knew him only by description and reputation. He was then asked if he knew personally that the two men had lived together. He could only answer, "No."

The magistrate then asked Estes if a witness who did personally know him could be sent for. This man would then be asked the above questions. After thinking for a time, and after some consideration, Estes related to the court that this seemed an unnecessary delay, with the laws being numerous and tedious. The court pointed out other similar cases, and Estes soon realized that bringing over someone who knew the prisoner was not such a bad idea after all.

Estes replied that such a man could be found and sent for.

John was then allowed to tell his side of the story. He informed the court that as he came into the cheese factory on the night before his trip to Switzerland, he discovered Christen murdered. Fearing he would be accused of the crime, he decided to flee after attempting to conceal all traces of the crime.

He went on to admit that he had made a big mistake by taking with him the things belonging to the murdered man.

John was then remanded and sent back to the custody of his jailors. It was at this time that he first learned that he was accused of murder.

Kuhni was back in prison, waiting for someone from Wisconsin to arrive so the extradition process could proceed.

❧

Back in Wisconsin, Governor Hoard received a cablegram from the American minister, Mr. Phelps, at London, stating that a person personally acquainted with John Kuhni, the murderer, would have to be sent to London to positively identify the fugitive before he could be extradited to the States. Because Sheriff Estes had never personally seen Kuhni, another person who could identify the man was needed in London. A local Dane County man would have to be selected to testify before the court in London, which meant more taxpayer expense for Dane County.

All Wisconsin newspapers reported similar articles as below which appeared in the *Ashland Weekly News* at Ashland, WI:

MUST GO TO ENGLAND
SOMEONE TO BE SENT THERE
TO IDENTIFY KUHNI

The Dane County Murderer held in London but will not be surrendered until he is recognized by an agent to prove his identity

Undersheriff Lea of Dane County, stationed in Madison, started immediately for the town of Primrose and returned with Peter H. Sangesand, carrying a traveling bag. Peter was a good choice because he was acquainted with John Kuhni and was willing and able to travel to Europe for the state. He also knew all the circumstances leading up to the crime and regarding the discovery of the body.

Sangesand was quickly awarded a commission from Governor Hoard and left immediately for Washington, D.C., where he would receive the next necessary papers and embark on Wednesday, January 9, from New York on a North German Line steamer to England.

Chapter Twelve
Estes—Sheriff,
Agent Marshall, & Tourist

The following is a narration of The *Wisconsin Democrats* interview with Estes on February 9, 1889, after returning back to Wisconsin.

Agent Estes now had many days on his hands with nothing to do. What was he to do in a strange city with no friends? He soon discovered that there was much to see in the city of London, and he decided to first satisfy his curiosity about the police system in that city.

He discovered that there were sixteen police courts in the London municipality, each conducted almost the same way that similar courts are managed on this side of the pond, as the Atlantic Ocean was called. Or, more appropriately, our courts were fair copies of theirs.

Flags are rarely seen in English courts. It is most common for the Royal Coat of Arms to be placed above and behind the judge, or presiding magistrate, although, in the city of London Magistrates' Court, a sword, flanked by the arms of the city and the Crown, stands vertically behind the judge.

Estes noticed that there was a considerable difference, however, in the arrangement of London's courtrooms and ours. The prisoner was kept standing in an iron cage called the prisoner's dock. The witness testifies from a canopied box, which looks, from a short distance, much like a single-top buggy. The location of the witness stand at the rear of the courtroom in London's famous Old Bailey courtroom is unlike the typical location of an American witness stand which is close to our judge's bench.

Very narrow slips, or pews, are provided for officers, reporters, and solicitors. Advocates usually speak standing up, not far from where they are seated. There is rarely any space for them to move, in any case. The London lawyer, when he addresses the court, rises straight up, stands still, and quietly talks or pleads his case with little effort or oratory.

Estes wondered how any of the lawyers he knew back in Madison would handle themselves in one of those narrow, strait-laced, lame-back, London solicitor's pews. Estes could easily envision the Wisconsin lawyer warming up to his subject. Then, waiting until his eyes began to blaze, he would then allow his eloquence to come thundering forth. Estes could see great beads of sweat beginning to chase each other down his perspiring countenance, sealing the fate of the hampering furniture.

He decided that one or the other would certainly perish in such a conflict. London solicitor's seats and Wisconsin's tragic oratory could never exist in the same place at the same time. In London, the narrow seats survive; in Madison, the oratory. In either case, he decided, it was the survival of the fittest.

He also noticed, to his horror, that the old practice of kissing the Bible while being sworn in still prevailed in London. During each day, several hundred people from the streets, from both the slums and from the city's higher walks of life, kissed the same book in about the same spot each time.

He later reported, "I had taken the oath in this ancient manner several times, and each time the thought had occurred to me: If this book is truly the most read book in history, it was definitely the most kissed book! And, definitely, the dirtiest."

He also noted that upon examination of one particular Bible, it was very evident that some person who had just kissed the book had recently been eating onions and also perhaps garlic.

During those days of waiting and to fill his time, London's detectives took him most any place he desired, and he was treated with the highest respect and courtesy all during his stay. He spent much of this time on the streets of London as a tourist, just watching the people: the weary worker trudging home from the blacking factory, the newshawk on the corner, the flower girl, the cabbie dozing on his hack parked by the curb, the horse's head drooping. He especially noticed the night fog, a common event, and the yellow glow of the streetlamps. One day they took him to Southampton, about seventy miles to the south, to enjoy and observe that city.

Mr. Gallagher, the editor of the *London Sport*, arranged to take Agent Estes to Dublin, but something transpired to prevent the trip. Estes said he could have had the run of half of England, but decided it was better to remain near his prisoner, for fear of something turning up or going wrong with the case. He was not about to take any chances.

❧

Two weeks to the day after proceedings were first filed against Kuhni in London; the requested depositions arrived from America. They were immediately handed over to Sir James Ingham. After reading them, Ingham related to Agent Estes that he did not need the witness who had been requested from Wisconsin, as there was sufficient testimony to secure the prisoner's commitment without him. But that witness, Peter Sangesand, Estes told him, was already en route, and was to arrive in port the next day aboard the steamer *Elba*. It was decided to wait for Sangesand; what was one more day?

When Sangesand arrived in London for the purpose of identifying John Kuhni, John was called from his cell. As John walked down the hall, Peter confronted him and called out his name. "John," he yelled. John paid no attention to the man approaching him. "Why, John, don't you recognize me?" said Peter. John, again, did not reply. Again, Peter spoke, and this time John said, "I suppose you came from America."

The two conversed for a few minutes. Peter, knowing he was there to identify the man, explained to the officials how John had previously broken his wrist, which was clearly visible to all. He continued, "Some time ago, John had taken a horse from the premises where Peter was employed and rode off with it. He was soon thrown from the horse and sustained the fracture at that time."

The final examination hearing in England was held on January 29, 1889. At this time, the Swiss Consul explained that he had communicated with his country and found that the fugitive had been twice under a penal sentence for stealing. He also made it unmistakably clear that Switzerland was not particularly desirous of receiving John back there—under any circumstances.

It was determined by the judge that the accumulated evidence was complete, and the prisoner was committed at once.

But, the United States had not, as yet, gained custody of the prisoner. According to the extradition treaty with Great Britain, the prisoner had fifteen days in which to appeal his case to a higher court. This could be dragged out almost indefinitely. Estes was very concerned when he learned this information.

However, John's attorney in London, Mr. Arthur Newton, who was now convinced of the prisoner's guilt, very generously agreed to drop the case. However, he did have to persuade John to personally request that he be sent back to America at once. This he was able to do. John agreed to return to the United States after learning that he could not, under any circumstances, return to Switzerland. He knew he had no other alternative; there was no place else for him to go.

Chapter Thirteen
Returns to Wisconsin

The *Madison Democrat* reported on February 19, 1889:

Two days later, on January 31, 1889, the party of three from Wisconsin was able to leave England for the United States. They traveled on the SS Britannic, *an ocean liner of the White Star Line, and the first of three ships of the White Star Line to sail with the Britannic name.*

The *Britannic*, a fast-moving steamship, was equipped with sails built for the White Star Line's North Atlantic run. The *Britannic* sailed for nearly thirty years, primarily carrying immigrant passengers on the highly trafficked Liverpool-to-New York City route.

In May of 1887, the *Britannic* had collided with another White Star liner, the SS Celtic, in thick fog about 350 miles east of New Jersey. Six steerage passengers were killed outright on board the *Britannic*, and another six were later found to be missing, having been washed overboard. There were no deaths on board the *Celtic*.

Two-and-a-half-year-old Eleanor Roosevelt was on board the *Britannic* at the time of the collision, with her father, Elliott, mother, Anna, and aunt Tissie. Eleanor was lowered into a lifeboat, screaming and protesting. She and her parents were taken to the *Celtic* and eventually returned to New York. Eleanor retained a lifelong fear of water and ships as a result of this incident.

Agent Estes reported that the trip back was very peaceful, and Kuhni gave them no trouble throughout the voyage. At once, he realized that there was no need to keep the prisoner in shackles, and they were not placed on his hands until they neared the shoreline of New York.

"Kuhni smokes steadily, eats heartily, but does not feel any remorse for what he did." It is reported that he did the crime for a paltry $100.

It was only at that time that he became very restless; noticed by Estes, it appeared very evident that John did not like to be in irons.

The group would have disembarked at Castle Garden on February 16, after sixteen days on the ocean. Castle Garden was established as an immigration station in 1855 to process immigrants pouring into New York. Prior to its establishment, passengers could disembark at any available dock without inspection or registration.

The morning the ship entered Manhattan Bay, an onlooker onshore might have noticed a strange sight or two onboard the liner. There were hundreds of people on deck, and it would have seemed to the onlooker as though every European town and village, every hillside, had been deserted in the race for America. This onlooker would have seen the happy and excited looks on the passengers' faces as they realized they were at their journey's end. These men and women from Europe, parents with excited children in their arms, each craning to see around the others, were getting their first look at America.

Herded eagerly onto the limited deck space, they rushed to the rails to get their first glimpse of America.

These tired, bedraggled people had been brought across a large ocean; they were families, lots of babies, and alas, each had little baggage! It was a mass of hundreds of unwashed people tugging at grimy bundles. The parents' faces were tired and undernourished.

Estes and Sangesand would have had that same look of excitement on their faces; they had been away from their families long enough. But that was not the case with John; he was headed for jail.

This group would not have had to go through the third-class immigration lines; they would be allowed to leave the ship immediately.

The journey to Wisconsin was by train and on the train, from New York City to Madison, Estes and Kuhni were shackled together, and according to Estes, they became close companions. Slowly the Northwestern train moved westward into the Wisconsin winter, jolting over crumbling roadbeds and shaky bridges as it moved closer toward its destination with each passing hour.

Once, during the trip, a traveler struck up a conversion with John, speaking in the German language. Estes had forbidden John to talk to anyone regarding the actual crime, but he agreed to permit him to visit casually with people. John was overheard telling the traveler about what he was accused of, and Estes decided to allow the conversation to continue as he was also very interested in hearing what John had to say about why he did the crime. He felt that John was more apt to tell a stranger about the facts, rather than to a sheriff. At one time, John was heard to say that Christen was like his brother; he had been a loyal friend. He also said that he could never kill a true friend and that he had made a mistake in leaving the country.

Then when the train neared Wisconsin, John became so nervous that the sweat stood out in great beads on his face. Later, Estes discovered that along with not liking to be in irons, John also did not like pressing through a large gathering of people, apparently fearing personal violence.

But, most of all, Estes especially noticed that John did not appear to show any remorse for the crime he was accused of doing at all.

Chapter Fourteen
Kuhni Safe in Jail

Six weeks after the crime, and four and a half weeks after Agent Estes had left for England, the party of Kuhni, Estes, and Sangesand arrived back in Madison. It was February 18, 1889. This was a big day for Estes, as he had not seen his family for a long time and he was also proud that he had fulfilled a job for his county.

John Estes, Sheriff and United States Marshall, was born in Milwaukee County, Wisconsin, on March 1, 1842, to Elijah and Z. Wentworth Estes, natives of North Carolina and Maine, respectively. Elijah had become a resident of Wisconsin in 1835 and was probably one of the first men to settle here.

John was the third of nine children and was reared on a farm in what later became the 17th Ward of Milwaukee. He attended three years at Beloit College and one year at the University of Wisconsin.

He enlisted as a private in Company A, Twenty-Third Wisconsin Regiment, in 1862. He served until the end of the Civil War and left the service as a lieutenant. After the war, he began to farm in Dunkirk Township, Dane County, and eventually became a wealthy man.

He was elected sheriff of Dane County in 1886. He later obtained considerable renown by following the murderer Kuhni to England, where he secured his extradition and brought him back to suffer the extreme penalty of the laws of the state of Wisconsin.[10]

An item about the Dane County sheriff's department, published in 1996, covered some of the days after John Kuhni's incarceration. Mr. Houghton, a Dane County deputy, recalled that there were times when not much was going on in Dane County requiring the sheriff's attention and that during those times, the only thing the sheriff did was take care of the jail and serve papers.

Houghton mentioned a time when a murder occurred in Dane County when Estes was sheriff: "That was a time when things became very active for the sheriff. He went on to relate how a guy had taken an ax and chopped up his employer in the town of Primrose. The events of this crime and later tracking the murderer to Europe and extradition process of getting him returned to Madison made the affair one of international notoriety." Estes considered that case to be one of the hardest times for himself, all during his time as serving as sheriff.

It has never been easy to keep a secret in a city, especially if the secret concerns mischief. Publicity should be a form of social cleansing and if any wrong was done, it was as though it must have been done not just to individuals, but to the community as a whole. The residents of Madison were no different and felt they had a right, a duty, to hear of the deed, to mark the wrongdoer,

---

[10] History of Dane County Wisconsin

to accept his atonement, and to pray for his healing.

On that cold Wisconsin Sunday night, when the train moved into the Madison station, the citizens of Madison and Dane County were waiting for the ex-sheriff and his prisoner.

The party of three had reached New York City after a trip of eighteen days on the ocean and arrived in Madison at 3:30 a.m. on the eighteenth on the Northwestern passenger train from Chicago. According to one newspaper, several hundred curious people awaited the train.

However, the train stopped several blocks away from where the train was supposed to have stopped at Angleworm Station at the South Carroll Street crossing. This station was a boat landing at the foot of State Street. Quickly debarking were three men, Estes, Kuhni, and Peter Sangesand, who walked to the jail with no one knowing they were back in town.

Here the prisoner was turned over to Sheriff Vernon, who warmly greeted the three men. The ex-sheriff, Estes, headed for home to see his family, from whom he had been so long separated.

John was now behind bars in Wisconsin, and subject to tormenting rats. A *Milwaukee Journal* reporter stated that Kuhni's quarters were no different from those of the other fifty-odd tramps who were also confined in the old rattletrap jail.[11]

The following newspaper article, printed the next day, states:

John Kuhni did not sleep an instant that night, so say the other prisoners, for they heard him for three or four hours talking in a strange tongue to somebody, or something. They could not understand a word of it. Later, laughing about it, they said that the rats had quite a lecture that night.[12]

Wisconsin State Journal Heading, Monday, February 18, 1889, followed by my summary:

AFTER MANY DAYS
Kuhni, the Alleged Murderer of William Christen, in the Town of Primrose, is Brought Back to Answer for His Crime

News of Kuhni's arrival in the city spread quickly. No one knows how, but by breakfast time on the eighteenth, a great many people, especially the young lads of the city who had missed his entrance the night before, had already learned that Kuhni was back in Wisconsin and in the local jail.

In the early 1800s, court proceedings were major social

---

[11] *Milwaukee Journal,* 23 Feb. 1889

[12] *Madison Democrat,* 19 Feb. 1889

events. During the 1880s and 1890s, it was common, both in the United States and in England, for people to come in off the streets to observe courtroom proceedings. I find this to be very unusual, but it is definitely true. Maybe it was because people had more time, more people were out of work, or perhaps many had servants who handled their day-to-day work.

Many curious spectators would climb the winding stairs to the courtroom to watch the great legal minds of the day represent their clients with skill, dedication, and a complete mastery of their profession.

The spectators, on this cold morning of February 18, 1889, were very disappointed that they had missed Kuhni's arrival at the train station. They complained that Sheriff Estes had been very sneaky, as he escorted John from the train to the jail without a soul noticing.

That morning, arising from their beds, they scrambled for their warm boots, coats, and scarves, some going without breakfast, hell-bent on getting a glimpse of Kuhni. Those curious folks anticipated action in the courthouse, and they were not going to miss it. With a typical case, the prisoner would have been hauled in from the jail, marched in front of the judge, and sent back to his cell with hardly anyone knowing what was going on. But this morning was going to be different, and everyone knew it. They were not going to miss this circus.

Just as soon as John Joy, the faithful janitor at City Hall, opened the doors of the municipal court on Monday morning, in pushed the multitude. "I guess the word is already out about this man," said John Joy. It was freezing in the room, as no one had started a fire yet, but nobody cared; they had a seat and every front seat was taken before John Joy had time to shake down the stove and dust off the chairs and tables.

Reporters had arrived from all over the state to report on the killer everyone was talking about and the melodrama in Madison. Earlier that morning, curious people made several attempts to get a close look at Kuhni through the iron bars of his cell. But Sheriff Vernon would not admit anyone, and visits were allowed only under the eye of an officer, making it impossible for anyone to talk to him. When the press finally got a look at Kuhni, he refused to look at them, turning his head downward. It was reported that his face was like that of a dead man, showing no emotion at all.

John was twenty-six years old. He spoke only broken English. He was five feet six with a light complexion and hair. He had a very thin, fuzzy mustache, and the prominent bridge of his nose had a scar across it. His hair was cut short, and a large scar showed across the back of his head. His right wrist was enlarged from a break that had never properly healed, and his ears were pierced for earrings, which he sometimes wore.

In the courtroom, anxiously waiting to get this over with, was Chief District Attorney John Erdall. Erdall had been elected as district attorney for Dane County for one term, which he served from 1888 to 1891. In 1895, he would become the assistant attorney general for the state of Wisconsin. In 1901 he became an attorney for the Chicago Great Western Railway. As the D.A., he was used to handling wife beaters and horse thieves, but this day appeared to be different. He decided it could be a useful challenge for him, possibly raising his profile and his chance for a higher position. He hoped that Kuhni's trial would be diverse and challenging, as he was used to making up rules on the fly, and he was seldom challenged by the law.

John Erdall was ready, excited, and anxious for the day.

A summary from articles in the *Wisconsin State Journal* and the *Madison Democrat,* February 19, 1889:

That morning, the eager crowd had a long wait. It was 9:10 before the prisoner arrived, Sheriff Vernon and Jailer Currier in charge of the prisoner. It was extremely difficult for anyone to press through the large and noisy crowd that blocked their way.

Everyone wanted a look at the demented, Dracula type person by the name of John Kuhni. He would surely be six feet tall with large hands, large enough to overtake his roommate. He would have the eye of a raven, a hawk, or an eagle with features like a meat ax.

Their staring eyes searched the room, their mouths gaping, looking for a murderer. But, when they soon discovered which person in the room was the vicious killer, it turned out to be that little fellow seated next to Sheriff Vernon. Some whispered, "Why, he isn't any bigger than the sheriff, five feet six inches in height and not very wide around!" Many in the crowd thought—"Well, fooled again!"

The appearance of Kuhni in the courtroom certainly did not meet the expectation of the crowd. That weeping piece of misery sitting up front was below the medium size of a man with no ferocious cast of countenance. His face was of a rather peculiar shape with a wide jaw, cheeks sunken, forehead receding. His mustache was a very slim excuse, of light color; on his chin were but few hairs with no side whiskers—never did have any to all appearances.

Could this man really be the murderer? Could he be capable of such a horrible crime as they had been reading and hearing about?

However, if one looked closely, it was very noticeable that his eyes were strange, appeared to have no life in them and no soul behind them or anywhere nearby.

He appeared to be dressed well, wearing a good suit of a hand-me-down coat, pants and vest, and a substantial overcoat. One gentleman in the courtroom, who was viewing Kuhni, and knew both the accused and the murdered man, whispered to the reporter: "That suit which Kuhni wears was William Christen's suit.

By and by, after multiple asking for the room to be silent, the court announced the case of the state against Kuhni. Presiding over the court as the Judge was the Honorable Mr. Stewart.

Sheriff Vernon stepped up to the prisoner, and in a kindly manner, said: "John, step up here before the court." John obeyed. The court asked: Have you any attorney?

The prisoner appeared excited, and his face was ashy pale. He made no reply.

District Attorney Erdall stepped up and spoke: Have you a lawyer? There was a shake of the head, and a low reply, "no, I no understand English."

The court requested Mr. R. G. Siebecker, attorney, to address the prisoner in German. Mr. Siebecker did so, and the reply from John was: "I have no lawyer; no money, but I can get some money from my brother."

"Where is your brother? Is he the one in the town of Primrose?" The prisoner nodded, yes.

Then the court was informed by another person who appeared to be well known with the family, stated that the brother would have nothing to do any further with the matter.

The court then directed Mr. Martin Hinriebe to ask the prisoner if he would be satisfied with Mr. Siebecker. Kuhni nodded, yes.

The attorney appointed to represent John was Robert Siebecker, born in Sauk County, Wisconsin. He had been admitted to the bar in 1879 and married Josephine La Follette, a sister to Senator Robert La Follette. They had both been born and raised in the township of Primrose, very close to where the crime was committed.

Robert Siebecker was the Madison City Attorney at this time. Mr. J. L. O'Connor, ex-district attorney, was appointed to assist District Attorney John Erdall in the case.

The court asked the District Attorney when he could have his case prepared, after consideration, he said on the 21st. The Judge set Saturday the 23rd at 9 a.m. in the morning for the preliminary examination.

When he returned to the jail, Kuhni was locked in one of the coops. After a while, he was permitted to walk in the hall, however, well-guarded, and allowed to smoke a pipe for a brief period each day. He was heard chatting a little, in broken English, on various subjects, but not a word was spoken by him of the crime charged against him.

❧

The court reports go on to state that if Kuhni pleads not guilty when he next appears, on Saturday the 23rd, an examination will be held. If he is held for trial, he will be remanded to the county jail awaiting trial in April before Judge Stewart, of the Dane County Circuit Court. If he pleads guilty, he will receive sentencing from the honorable Judge Stewart.

There were all kinds of speculations regarding what course the prisoner would take. So far, he had shown no signs of admission or confession of guilt.

❧

The *Wisconsin State Journal* published an article on January 21, 1889, about the condition of the Dane County Jail. The paper reported:

Wisconsin is well provided with means to punish even the worst sort of its criminals. If the state took over the Dane County Jailhouse, which is a stone pile, to use for murderers in the first degree and put them in there for five years, it would be equal to death, especially for butchers like Kuhni. We predict that after five years in that building, when let out, any man, if still alive after inhaling nothing but the foulest of air and fighting with such an army of insects and vermin for that length of time, if not dead by then, would definitely take up religion.

Kuhni's cell was small, about the size of a walk-in closet, with a narrow cot and one thin blanket. It was musty and cold, as very little heat entered the rows of cells from the wood stove nearby. On January 14, the weather was thirty degrees below zero—again. Roads were blocked with snow, and the snow's crust was frozen so hard that teams of horses could not walk upon it.

The newspapers mentioned that fences were being used for firewood, and provisions were becoming scarce. Lake Monona, in Madison, succumbed to the cold and was closed from shore to shore, a very unusual event.[13]

The murder of Christen and the case against John Kuhni continued to attract considerable attention throughout the state, and the citizens of Dane County excitedly awaited the trial.

____

[13] *Madison Democrat*, 14 Jan. 1890

Chapter Fifteen
Before the Court

The headline of the *Madison Democrat* on Saturday, January 24, 1889, read:

The Jam on Sat morning, at the Municipal Court to see Kuhni, the alleged Murderer

The below account of the day is based on the reporting of several Madison newspapers and narrated in my words:

Old-timers remember when Barnum, in his best of days, traveling with his huge show—there was always a great jam at the gates with everyone anxious to see Mr. Barnum and to purchase a ticket for the great show.

The jam on Saturday morning, at the municipal court, in the hall to the courtroom and all down the stairs of City Hall to the Mifflin street front door, equaled any jam that Barnum ever saw in this region. P.T. Barnum would place himself near the ticket office to please the crowd. However, Kuhni is no more like Barnum than Hamlet to Hercules, and yet the jam at municipal court equaled any jam that Barnum ever saw.

Everybody appeared to be anxious to see Kuhni, yes, and the crowd filled the sidewalk in front of the city hall very early that day. There were an unaccountable number of bodies and faces, hats and bonnets, their noses red and cheeks raw from the biting January wind. They began to jam closer and closer together, bound by a single determination to get in or at least to see the spectacle that was about to occur.

The most significant jam was at 9 a.m. The police were accustomed to the management of crowds, and a few officers tried to hold the multitude back. However, they knew these people were only here for a taste of novelty and spectacle and felt that they deserved to have their time and fun. Winter was getting long for everyone and because they did not want to spoil anyone's fun, they did not try very hard to control the crowd.

With 16,000 people living in Madison at this time, it seemed as though one half of the population was in front of the city hall that morning, according to one reporter.

The county courthouse in the 1800s was a foundation of the community, social life, and tradition. Historically, courthouses were found in the center of towns, where people could easily observe the law in action. Outside, the public celebrated holidays and picnicked on the lawn and set off fireworks as they celebrated the Fourth of July holiday.

Today, citizens don't visit their courthouses unless compelled to do so and trials are not of interest to most. Today the people and the newspapers are more interested in celebrities than they are in trials.

❧

Within a few minutes Sheriff Vernon and Jailer Currier, with their prisoner Kuhni, arrived in a cutter and very cleverly entered the City Hall door on the Wisconsin Avenue side of the building, not the main entrance door. Quickly, before anyone could see them, they slipped up the stairs and into the courtroom, with only a few knowing of this.

Inside, the courtroom was packed to suffocation, with a crowd morbidly curious to obtain a view of Kuhni. Most had been there since the doors opened several hours ago.

It was with the most utmost difficulty for the lawyers, officers, and Judge Stewart to press through the jam in the courtroom to get to their proper places. Many in the crowd were not happy, and they showed their disappointment when they again learned that they had missed the opportunity to view the murderer up close.

However, when the party reached the bar, Judge Keyes announced that the examination in the case had been delayed until next Friday morning, March 1.

The vast crowd outside the room showed their disappointment with yells and booing. But when information went forth that the examination in the case would take place in the circuit courtroom in Dane County courthouse next Friday morning, March 1 at 10 a.m., the crowd appeared somewhat satisfied and settled down. Rufus Smith was retained to assist R. J. Siebecker in defense of the accused.

Then the sheriff and jailer quickly ushered the prisoner from the room, moving through the crowd with aid from the Chief of Police, Adamson, who forcefully broke the way for them.

The party moved very fast down the stairway and out the Wisconsin door before boarding the cutter. They proceeded to get away so quickly that the people, still straining their necks to look over the heads of those in front, did not have a chance to view the action.

The *Milwaukee Journal* reported on February 18, 1889:

Before the prisoner was escorted to court, which happened in the afternoon, several attempts have been made to get a look at the prisoner through the bars of the cell. Sheriff Vernon is not disposed to gratify idle curiosity and does not admit anyone but members of the press. Kuhni has not said one word, on the advice of his lawyers. All visitors are under the eye of an officer, and consequently, it is impossible to have a visit with him.

When seen this morning, he was lying upon a crude couch but raised to a sitting position as I approached. He wore a hang-dog look as if desiring to avoid recognition. He glanced toward me and then turned his head downward.

February of that year was a vicious month, with temperatures dropping to twenty below at night and rising only to negative thirteen during the day, although with lots of sunshine.

Along with the miserable weather, Wisconsin had its share of butchers that winter. On February 20, an article in the *Madison Democrat* mentioned:

There is another butcher in Wisconsin, who is almost as bad as the Dane County butcher, Kuhni.

Louis Burk, of High Bridge, near Ashland, decided

that his wife was on too friendly of terms with Thomas Montgomery. Louis chopped up his victim with an ax while he was asleep. The butcher stole away to Mellon and then surrendered to the deputy sheriff.[14]

95

---

[14] *Madison Democrat*, 20 Feb. 1889

Chapter Sixteen
Again, in Court

The murder of Christen and the case against John was still attracting considerable attention throughout the state, and the citizens of Dane County excitedly awaited the trial. On March 2, the *Madison Democrat* delivered the following headlines about the examining trial that had been held the day before:

Kuhni on Examination
Which John Kuhni has Never
Been Held to Account for
Examined Before the Municipal Court and Held for
Trial Which Will be Had Before the Dane Circuit Court

Material for the following account is based on the reporting of three different newspapers that covered the trial: the *Madison Democrat*, the *Wisconsin State Journal*, and the *Milwaukee Journal*. I have narrated events in my words, based on information reported in all three papers. The proceedings were expected to be sensational, and they did not disappoint.

As early as 8 a.m. on March 1, 1889, hundreds of people—old men, young boys, and girls—flooded the sidewalks in front of the county jail. People with morbid curiosity, people without work, people who didn't really know what brought them there, all assembled there two hours early. The doors of the circuit courtroom were not open until 10 a.m. because the municipal court was in session at the City Hall until that hour.

The courthouse was jammed with people milling in the halls, and when the doors were opened, what a rush there was for front positions—only a few seats were open, and, as it always happened, the biggest and tallest managed to arrive first for the best seats. This left the shorter people standing behind the taller ones, and so unable to see well. Many were attempting to find seats in a courtroom that could not hold a tenth of the people who wanted seats.

Some brought their lunch and dinner so they would not have to give up their seats once they found one.

Judge Keyes made his way to the circuit courtroom at precisely 10 a.m. He had studied the case in-depth and was up to date on the history of events. No one in Dane County could have been unaware of the horrible murder. Keyes had already talked to the D.A. and all the lawyers. So far, the day had been just a typical day in court consisting of routine matters, mostly civil suits. But, as the doors opened and the crowd began pressing in, Judge Keyes sat up and took great attention as he recognized that this would not continue to be a normal day for anyone, especially him.

Sheriff Vernon and his jailer, Currier, appeared with the prisoner, entering from the rear of the building. They had to press through the huge crowd, which again packed the stairway and corridors, then through the judge's room, to a final position within the bar of the courtroom. Jailer Currier was guarding the prisoner very closely, as some observers became rowdy and were displaying hostility toward the defendant.

The courtroom became busy as the lawyers and witnesses began to arrive. Other parties began to bring in armfuls of evidence to display for the court. Among those items was a bloody ax and a two-foot stick of stove wood smeared with blood. There was also a gun, lock, with stock detached; a washtub with blood marks inside and out with hair visible in the blood, bloody clothes and a bloody bag. These things were all laid down in front of the witness stand for all to see.

Fifteen to twenty witnesses took their places on each side of the bar.

Most defendants have some personal support in court, but this time there appeared to be no one; John was noticeably alone. No one, not even his only brother in America, was there to support him. He appeared rather pale and thin from his confinement but showed scarcely any evidence of excitement or remorse.

When the court was called to order, District Attorney Erdall announced that the complaint had been amended to replace the name Hans with John. John Kuhni was accepted by the court as the defendant's name.

District Attorney Erdall and ex-District Attorney O'Connor appeared for the prosecution. Kuhni was represented by an able array of legal talent, namely, City Attorney R. J. Siebecker and his partner, S.A. Harper, the Honorable Rufus Smith and his partner, the Honorable C. E. Buell.

Mr. Siebecker, John's attorney, had been elected city attorney in 1886 and would again be elected in 1890. This was his first murder trial, and he was somewhat nervous about how he would handle things. After this trial, Governor Hoard would appoint him judge, and he would later become Chief Justice of the Wisconsin Supreme Court. His reputation would show him to be a wise and just judge and known to have a deep sense of human rights.

∽

The first witness for the state was Peter Sangesand, the young man who had traveled to England to identify the prisoner. After taking his seat and being sworn in, he told of how he knew the two men, Kuhni and Christen. They had been his neighbors and said he was also acquainted with the cheese factory where the murder occurred.

He described how he and Nels Holland went to the factory on December 11, 1888, when Kuhni showed Peter a new gun and a workshop he had made in the basement of the factory. He went again on December 13 when they had noticed smoke and a terrible odor in the air. They knew something was wrong but could not detect where it was coming from at the time.

They had gone first to Anderson's barn, another neighbor, thinking the fire was there, but soon realized the smell was coming from the cheese factory. When they arrived, they went directly to the cellar door, where they saw smoke coming from the basement; they found the door locked. They told the court that after pounding on the door and asking to be let in, Kuhni soon opened the door for them to enter. They could barely see Kuhni for the smoke coming from behind him. They found the room full of smoke, and it had the smell of hair and meat burning.

When asked where Christen was, John replied, "Upstairs." Peter said they did not stay long because "it was a nasty place, smelly, and Kuhni could not speak English."

Peter was also questioned about trouble Kuhni had had with another cheesemaker. He related that he knew John to have previously been in trouble with a man named Samuel Wilkins at Peterson's Cheese Factory, a nearby factory, in August or September of last year.

He described the two men, Christen and Kuhni, as he had known them. The defense then questioned him about the distance from his home to the factory and the exact measurements of the factory. He was also asked for the precise arrangement of the rooms in the factory.

He identified the cheese factory building in detail and described finding two small bones in the ashes of the fire that had smelled so horribly and said the remains of chickens and wild game were found in different places around the factory, which meant that these bones were probably game bones. The men often went hunting for food, he said.

He told of returning to the factory on December 21, to help identify parts of an unidentified body found in the river near the factory. He told the court he immediately identified the remains of William Christen.

Peter was then asked to describe the scene of the murder. The courtroom was dead silent as Sangesand began to describe the murder scene in detail. The room was so quiet one could hear a pin drop as he described the blood on the walls, which appeared to have been covered with ashes or ink. He described finding a stick of wood, also covered with blood.

At this time, the stick was presented to the court, along with a bloody tub, which was identified as having been found in the factory. The container was brought forward and examined. Human hair could be seen still clinging to it.

Sangesand noted that the hair was the same color as Christen's. He was asked how he could know that the hair was not from an animal. He replied, "Because I cut hair for the neighborhood boys, and I can recognize human hair from animal hair. That was no hair from any animal I know of."

Next, Sangesand, after being handed the ax, examined the bloody instrument and identified it as the one that had been found in the factory. "When I first saw the ax, there was blood and hair on it; the hair was the same as Christen's," he continued. "The area was covered with scattered bloody cheese covers, rugs, and rags probably used to wipe up the blood."

He was then asked to precisely identify marks on the head of the deceased when he had first seen it. He described the seven deep cuts in detail. There were six cuts on the head and one on the nose. The nose bone had been broken.

He described how investigators had searched for the remaining parts of the body but had found nothing. He explained how, at first, they had thought the small bones found in the furnace were human, but soon decided they were animal bones. A board had been discovered with blood and chicken feathers on it, but he explained that it was evident that much butchering of animals had previously taken place in the cellar.

He told the court that he suspected the body had not

been burned, explaining that it would have been no small task to destroy a human body by burning it. The act would require a certain kind of fuel, something like pine kindling because the fire would die out otherwise, and it would have taken a long time to completely destroy a body in that manner.

Sangesand was allowed to leave the stand.

⁓

J. J. Tschudy, the ticket agent from Monroe, was called at 2 p.m., after the break. He testified that on December 14, John had purchased tickets to Philadelphia, Queenstown, Liverpool, and the final destination of Basel, Switzerland. He also described the large roll of bills John had with him and how much John had paid for the tickets. Also, he discussed the best and fastest way to travel to Europe.

He was shown the satchels and confirmed, "Yes, they are like the ones Kuhni had carried that night."

The agent testified that he noticed at the time that John had carried two guns. He also said that a young man had accompanied John, and the two had discussed the best route for John to take. There was no indication of who this young man might be. (Perhaps it was the constable who had helped John with his bags.)

A constable who had ridden on the train from New Glarus to Monticello with Kuhni testified that he had helped the man place his two handbags upon his shoulder. He described noticing that his palm came away wet from thin, watery blood when he removed his hand from the bag. At the time, he thought Kuhni had rabbits in the bag, as he was carrying guns. Now, however, he testified that he believed one satchel held pieces of the missing body.

Peter Sangesand was again called to the stand to explain more fully the nature of the cuts on the head of the murdered man. He said he thought a sharp instrument had made one cut that went through the skull. He was also questioned in detail about a bedtick found hidden behind some shelving in the factory basement.

The Honorable P. O. Baker, a farmer, and member of the state legislature who lived in the township of Primrose about one and a quarter-mile from the factory, was next called to testify.

Baker said he knew Christen and had seen Kuhni several times. He had visited the factory many times when the men were present. When Baker had been called on December 21 to identify the body parts, he had immediately recognized the head as belonging to Christen.

His testimony was similar to Sangesand's regarding the viewing of the remains, the inquest, and the jurymen's examination of the factory and the immediate area. He explained that he thought the blood on the walls showed finger marks.

He identified the pieces of clothing found in the factory, and the bag, which had supposedly held the body parts. He mentioned that he had noticed some lettering on the bag reading H.U. &. P.Y. Wisc. It was concluded that the initials probably stood for Humphry, a local grain dealer.

In cross-examination, Baker described the cuts on Christen's head. He said some of them appeared to have been made by a sharp instrument, such as an ax. One cut had gone through the skull. He thought that any of the blows to the head were significant enough to kill a man.

All through this testimony, Kuhni listened but did not appear to be overly distraught. His face showed no emotion as if he did not hear the words spoken by the many witnesses who were testifying against him.

As the witnesses were being brought forward, sometimes returning again to the stand to tell more of what they knew, Judge Keyes had been watching the face of Kuhni.

He noticed the lack of emotion and thought: *God help us*, this man before me who has slaughtered his best friend, dismembered the body, is now showing no apparent remorse for his deeds. *What kind of a man is this?*

William Rea, the man who, with his brother, found the head in the bag, was called next. He told his story and related that he had not known either Christen or Kuhni before that day. He notably testified that the sack could not have floated down the river because of the small amount of water in the creek at the time.

P. G. Krogh, a Mount Horeb hardware merchant, testified that Kuhni and Christen had been in his store the day before the crime was supposed to have been committed. They had just drawn money on checks made out by Rudy Ragats, their employer.

Christen had drawn pay for the work of the season, and Kuhni for about a month's labor as an assistant. Krogh stated that he understood that Kuhni was employed to assist Christen at the factory. After cashing their checks, he noted, the two young men had looked over the supply of guns and revolvers he carried but did not purchase any.

⚶

Ex-Sheriff Estes was called to the stand. He testified at length about crossing the Atlantic Ocean, going to London, the arraignment of the prisoner, and bringing him back to Wisconsin.

He mentioned that John Kuhni was wearing the same suit of clothes he had on when Estes first met him in London. Kuhni's guns were at that time in possession of the police department in Liverpool, and Detective Froest in London was holding Kuhni's other possessions.

Estes slowly proceeded to remove each item, one by one, from the bag, explaining what each was. There were two watches, one clock, a pocketbook, two pairs of shoes, a razor, chains, a straw hat, a knife, and a thermometer.

Blood was found on one pair of shoes, and on the knife that had been found rolled up in some clothing. A certificate of application for U.S. citizenship for John Kuhni was shown to the court.

A bloodstained shirt was then removed from the bag, and a German singing book containing the name of William Christen on the flyleaf. "Yes," Estes said, "he brought everything back to the States with him, except for the guns." (I wonder if they were ever returned. There was also no mention of the missing photo.)

The evidence was judged admissible.

When asked by the lawyer how he got along with Kuhni during that time, Estes replied that Kuhni was a very calm and congenial passenger and when asked what John had said to him about the murder Estes replied that throughout the trip, John continued to deny killing his friend. "We were like brothers," John had told him. "How could I murder my brother?" John had told Estes he did not see any blood on the garments. (I am not sure of what garments he was referring to.)

Estes was asked if he had found any photographs of Kuhni in the luggage. He said he had not. "Perhaps he had destroyed them," he said.

At this point, there arose a dispute between the lawyers as to whether the defendant's imperfect understanding of the German language made him an incompetent witness.

Rudolf Ragats, the Mount Horeb cheesemaker who operated the Holland Cheese Factory, testified that he had paid Christen $137.68 on November 27 at the Ragats home in Mount Horeb. Christen and Kuhni had come to collect their pay for the season as there would be no more cheesemaking until next spring.

Rudy Ragats (spelled Regetz, Regez, or Ragats in the newspapers of the time, and later as Ragatz) operated six cheese factories in Dane County. He was the son of Jacob, who was still in Switzerland at this time and had a brother named Jacob. Rudy had come to this country about 1872. Another brother, Ernst, came over in 1880.

Ragats testified that the clock found in John's possession had come from his factory. The pocketbook, he said, looked like Christen's. He, himself, had purchased for Christen the suit and pair of shoes. The bloody vest, he explained, went with the suit. The vest was compared with the suit John now wore, and witnesses said it was a good match. Ragats had known Christen well and had paid him additional money during the summer and fall months. The knife was also recognized as Christen's. Ragats knew that William Christen had purchased a pair of shoes at a store in Mount Horeb, very much like those shown to him. Ragats had visited the factory frequently during the summer, and Christen was there often.

Throughout the trial, John seemed unconcerned about all of the brouhaha until he noticed someone familiar who had just entered the courtroom. It was his brother, Fritz, who passed John without a sign of recognition and took a seat in front of him, only twelve feet away. It was noticeable to everyone there that day that the prisoner had suddenly become very nervous. His lips became tightly drawn, and a quivering of the muscles of his neck was plainly visible. However, he soon recovered and composed himself once more.

Fritz Kuhni, brother of the accused, was then brought to the stand. He had been waiting in the hallway to be called to testify. Fritz told of John first working for him in his cheese factory, and then leaving to live with Christen.

Fritz further testified that his brother had come to Dane County the previous July with only a few cents to his name from Switzerland. Fritz had given John some work and paid him sixty dollars for three months. He knew John had purchased a gun with some of the money.

Fritz continued by relating his trip to New Glarus with John early in the morning on December 14. John had told him during the ride that he and Christen had accidentally shot a hog and thought they would be in trouble for it, and that Christen had gone ahead to New Glarus. Fritz had helped to load the satchels in the wagon. Both were very heavy, he said, and one was heavier than the other. Fritz and John had started out for New Glarus at about 5:30 a.m. They had not talked much except about shooting the hog. John had also mentioned to Fritz that he might go home to Switzerland.

Fritz had dropped John off at the depot in New Glarus and had looked through the passenger cars for William Christen, but could not find him. John had explained that Christen had probably gone ahead on the night train.

As Fritz left the depot to return home, and as the train began to move, John had come out onto the platform and asked his brother not to tell anyone he was leaving. Fritz testified that he had wondered at the time why John had not wanted anyone to know of his leaving, but that he had forgotten about it; at the time it did not seem important to him.

When the court asked about John's relationship with his parents in Switzerland, Fritz explained that John had not lived with his parents in Switzerland lately because his father did not like him.

Where did he live then, if not with his parents?

"I do not know; he was here and there."

John's parents lived in the canton of Bern with the post office address of Ursenbach. Fritz said he had a letter from his sister telling him John had been in prison for a time, perhaps in the fall of 1883.

John Estes was re-examined and testified more about his conversations with Kuhni. Estes explained that by the time the trip was coming to an end, he was able to get the drift of the German language that John was using and that John had consistently claimed to be innocent throughout the trip. Kuhni had continued to explain that Christen and he were like brothers and that he could not do such a thing to a brother.

John had told Estes that he was, however, present when the murder took place. The story from John's mouth, according to Estes, was that two strangers had entered the factory, knocked John down, murdered Christen, and left. John had explained that he thought the murder would be blamed on him, and therefore he tried to hide the evidence and leave the country.

Among the witnesses subpoenaed were Godfred Hageman and Paulina Kuhni, who, for an unknown reason, were not called to the stand. Paulina was the wife of Fritz. I have not been able to identify Godfred Hageman. He must have been a neighbor or a friend from Switzerland. Later, in 1916, a Carl Hageman married Anna Kuehni, a niece of John.

The prosecution rested, and the case was submitted. The court said: "There is no need to review the testimony. Murder has been committed, and there is probable cause to believe the defendant is guilty of such. The defendant is bound over for the next term of the Circuit Court of Dane County without bail."

Judge Stewart will hold the trial in the Dane County Circuit Court, at the next April term. John Erdall & J.L O'Connor will conduct the prosecution. The defense is R. Siebecker, assisted by R.B. Smith, S.A. Harper, and O.E. Buell.

All throughout the trial, pens, pencils, and inkwells were used to place every word spoken that day onto paper. The paper used was legal paper, yellow and lined, used especially for the recording of court trials. Those doing the writing must have had fingers that ached badly after scribbling so much information. Today there are laptops and tape recorders where once there were only pencils for notes and inkwells and ledgers to later record the documents.

As the reporters scrambled to leave the room, attempting to run each other over, some must have thought, "Wow! This is great material, good enough for the following edition. I must get out of here, fast." The next day there was a full-page covered with very small print about the trial proceedings of the previous day in the *Wisconsin State Journal* and the *Madison Democrat*.

The same papers reported that day that four tramps had been interrogated before the same judge and were given five days in the county jail on bread and water only, to which the first three agreed. The fourth man told the judge that "he could manage to propel his extremities out of the city, as the judge had ordered, and was quickly granted that privilege."

⋙

It came about that the trial was not held in April 1889, because the defense attorneys asked the court to delay the trial. The reason given was that they believed the sanity of the accused could not be impartially investigated in such a short time. They also needed the opinions of persons not living in this country. The attorney had written to friends and relatives of the defendant in Switzerland and to public officers in that country and was awaiting answers.

The trial was then set for November of 1889.

Major newspapers all across the United States, along with local and state papers, continued to report on the story. Publications including the *Chicago Tribune*, *New York Times*, *Minneapolis Star Tribune*, and *Boston Globe* all continued to print updates, though many of the reporters must have had a great sense of adventure because some of the stories were greatly embellished.

For instance, an article found in the *St. Paul Globe* on December 24, 1888, reported: "...concluded that the satchels held the deceased body of Christen and wondered why the murderer would attempt to carry the remains back to Switzerland."

The *Marion (Ohio) Star* headline on January 18, 1890, read: "...cuts out his black heart and murders an atheist to rid the world of him."

The *Boston Globe*'s December 31, 1888, headline reads: "Cheesemaker Christen Chopped to Pieces by his Swiss Companion," followed by "Most Horrible Homicide in Wisconsin History." The paper proceeded to cover the story in very small print with great detail.

A *Chicago Tribune* article headlined "Kuehni Brought Back" told how Wilhelm Christen, a Swiss cheesemaker who had settled in Dane County, had built a small cheese factory. (Not true.) It continues: "At the end of the cheesemaking season, he discharged all of the men except John Kuehne [sic]." It went on to say that Kuhni had told

Christen's brother (the reporter must have questioned an unknown brother, for this is the first of this conversation I have heard of) that his employer had closed the factory and gone away. John also related that Christen had had a quarrel with a neighbor and then left the area suddenly. (I have found none of this information in any of the local papers.)

The *Neenah (Wisconsin) Daily Times* of February 19 reported: "The murder was done for a paltry $100." Where did they get this figure? The paper also reported that Kuhni was a milk dealer.

On February 18,1889, the *Reading (Pennsylvania) Times* carried the following Page 1 headline:

TRACKED ACROSS THE SEA
The arrest of the Fiendish Wisconsin Murderer
Arrives at New York Yesterday
Kuehn's [sic] Bloody Crime to acquire
Money to visit his Swiss Home

The story filled two columns with very small print conveying information never seen in print before that day.

The long report changed many details formerly reported, such as:

...Kuehn went to town and returned with a gallon of whiskey and sat down with William to get drunk. When about one-half drunk, he ceased drinking himself but continued to refill Christen's glass until he was stupid.

Where did this information come from? The errors continued:

…Gathering an ax, he returned to the house where he found Christen on the floor and began to kill him with the ax.

…Taking the two satchels filled with the ghastly freight that he had packed and left for Monroe.

… finding the sack in the creek, the two boys ran home to tell their mother what they had discovered.

…Christen was reported to be a wealthy farmer!

…John's brother had supposedly met John on the road to Monroe… the brother congratulated John on his luck. (I doubt that.)

…The sheriff hastened there the same day that the sack was found.

…when pulled from the ship at Queenstown, John still had the two satchels but had thrown the body parts overboard.

What an imagination! The above statements were not reported elsewhere and were never proved to be true.

◆

On November 3, the lawyers obtained valuable evidence that at the time of the alleged murder, the defendant was insane and not responsible for his acts. They asked for more time to work on the new evidence.

November 15 arrived, and the jury was in the courtroom, ready for a trial. The attorneys of John Kuhni asked for another delay.

The defense said they could not, at that time, obtain sufficient evidence of insanity. Three doctors had examined John, and all three felt they needed more time to examine him, but initially felt he was indeed mentally imbalanced. They needed more time for the examination.

Judge Stewart continued the case to January 16, 1890, over the stubborn opposition of District Attorney Erdall and ex-District Attorney O'Connor, who declared that a continuance was unnecessary. They argued that nine months ought to have been sufficient time for the attorneys to prepare their case. It was an injustice to the taxpayers of the county, the men said, to compel them to pay double court expenses in this case without good reason. They went on to say that if there was adequate evidence of the man's sanity, the defense had had ample opportunity and plenty of time to prepare that case.

The defense attorneys reaffirmed their declaration that they needed more time because they had just received new evidence, which would take their case on a different route.

This was granted.

What was this new evidence?

During the past nine months, John had stuck to his story, as follows: While he and Christen were sleeping in the bedroom of the Holland factory, he was awakened by men pulling Christen from the bed. He also was taken, he said, bound hand and foot and dragged downstairs into the cellar. He fainted from the effects of violent treatment, and when he recovered, his partner was gone, and he was released. The men had held a revolver to his head and made him promise absolute secrecy. He noticed the bloodstains about the factory, and thinking he would be charged with the murder; he covered all traces of the crime as best he could and left for Switzerland.

❧

Another Christmas passed with no verdict, and John was still in jail. Was John guilty? If not, who was?

Time weighed heavily on John. He had no visitors, not even his brother, Fritz, who lived nearby. He had plenty of time to think about what he had done and what was going to happen to him.

Notwithstanding the improbability of his story, Kuhni would give no other account, and the theory of his defense must necessarily be that he did not commit the crime. This story was repeated to Sheriff Estes on the way back to Wisconsin from England and was afterward told to the state's counsel. For nine months, he adhered to this version of the event, stubbornly refusing to take anyone into his confidence.

During this time, Madisonites played ball, visited friends, went to work, and attended church. John bided his days in his cell. Surely, he wondered what was going to happen to him. He must have been secretly scared, frightened, and ashamed. However, in all these months, he stubbornly did not stray from his story.

During the November 1889 county board meeting, John Estes and Peter Sangesand were questioned by several board members about the bills the two had turned in for their trips overseas to bring John back to Wisconsin. The bills included interest. What was this interest, they were asked? In order to make the trip, they had to come up with the money themselves, which they had been told would be reimbursed to them later. Neither of these men had any extra money, let alone enough to take an expensive boat ride to England. They explained that they had to borrow the necessary funds from the German Bank. The county, according to the two men, should pay the interest on the loan. Expenses for Estes were $1,700 without the interest.

At first, the board refused to pay the interest of thirty-nine dollars for ex-Sheriff Estes and eleven dollars for Sangesand. "Due to the old fogyism of its members, the Primrose county board refused to allow the payment for the interest added by the bank. Mr. Estes could easily have made his expenses $300 or $400 higher, with no one questioning him, but he was not a man to do that, and like justice, to him, he felt he ought to be paid what he did ask for."[15]

After much discussion, the board did pay the entire bill for each man.

At the same meeting, Sheriff Vernon stated that he needed at least one more jail guard on hand at all times due to the "dangerous prisoner" confined there and that he considered the county insufficiently guarded. John Kuhni was the only prisoner held there for murder at the time, and as it was reported that his record of cooperation with the jailers was exemplary and that he caused no problems at all, the board members refused his request for extra help. Vernon was ordered to sit down.[16]

---

[15] *Oregon (Wisconsin) Observer,* 22 Nov. 1889

[16] *Madison Democrat,* 16 Nov. 1889

Chapter Eighteen
Pleads Guilty

Two months later, January 16, 1890, the *Wisconsin State Journal* newspaper headline reads:

KUHNI PLEADS GUILTY

What is this? When did this confession happen? Why suddenly a change in his story?

Remember back in November when his lawyers asked for more time because they had evidence the prisoner was insane? (This information will never come to light.)

The *Milwaukee Journal* on January 25, 1890, tells us:

It has been the theory of the counsel for the defense that Kuhni was insane when he killed Christen. Today, just prior to his court session, his two lawyers and a physician called at the jail to get the killer's story. This was when he made his first admission to the crime. This confession has been religiously guarded by those who received it, and until today, not even the fact that the murderer had told the story was known. His story is long and shows that he was a religious fanatic and that his crime was committed while laboring under religious excitement.

On Sunday, November 11, 1889, John confessed to the murder of his friend and co-worker to his lawyers and doctors, according to news reports and written statements by his lawyer and doctors. He had finally been convinced that, in Wisconsin, a guilty verdict would not be so horrible. Wisconsin had abolished the death penalty in 1853, and if convicted, Kuhni would have good board and comfortable lodging for the rest of his life. He had then opened up, spending hours relating the gory details. The witnesses reported that the story was so horrible and bloodcurdling, the details so gross that they doubted whether he was telling the truth. They later explained that they seriously thought his imagination was running riot.

It was this story that led the lawyers and his physicians, Fox, Gill, and Bodenius, to whom it was told, to suspect that Kuhni might have been insane—a suspicion that, however, had not been verified by many examinations.

After much consultation, they declared that the evidence against John, although entirely circumstantial, was so overwhelming that it was deemed best for him, with his own consent, to plead guilty, thus avoiding a long, tedious trial with only one inevitable termination—a verdict of guilty. With an appreciation of the horrors that the prosecution would bring forth and the effect and excitement that would have upon the prisoner, his counsel agreed to allow him to plead guilty before the court, asking that his appearance for that purpose be permitted before January 20. Accordingly, the time was set for eleven o'clock on the morning of January 16, 1890.

I have not discovered that any court sketchers were present at these trials, but they could have been there.

Since the Salem witch trials of 1692, over a century before the first photograph was snapped, artists have created sensitive and high-profile drawings for an eager public.

∽

The news broke in the *Wisconsin State Journal* on January 16 and in the *Madison Democrat* on January 17, 1890. The story covered an entire page of each paper in extra-small print. The below account is narrated in my words based on information from the two papers:

On January 16, 1890, John Kuhni was brought into court by Sheriff Vernon and Jailor Currier. They were also accompanied by ex-Sheriff Estes. The prisoner appeared pale and nervous, yet there seemed to be nothing brutish or villainous in his countenance, according to the reporters.

John appeared before Judge John R. Bennett, who was sitting with Judge Siebecker in the circuit court.

As he was brought in, District Attorney Erdall arose and said: "May it please the court, in the case of the state of Wisconsin against John Kuhni, I move that the defendant is arraigned (charged)."

The court: "Is the defendant in the room?"

Attorney Smith: "He is, your honor, but will require an interpreter." Mr. Herman Pfund was sworn as an interpreter who then read to the prisoner, interpreting the information of the District Attorney, charging him with willfully causing the death of William Christen.

Mr. Rufus Smith then told the court about the confession made the previous November and how John's attorneys had become convinced that the crime was the outcome of religious zeal.

❦

How and when did John's brother, Fritz, learn about the confession? We will never know. These details have not been handed down in our family. Evidently, Fritz and his wife never told their children about this "horrible" relative and what John had done to another human being. It had long been commonplace to conceal any evidence of an imperfect member of one's family from the public, or even other family members.

Lawyer Rufus Smith continues:

For one month prior to the date on which the murder was committed, December 12, 1888, John had been working and living with Christen at the factory. The two men apparently became fast friends during that month. William had come from Lemiswyl, the same area of Switzerland that John came from. Perhaps they knew each other from school or church. The Swiss immigrants do look out for one another, and the local cheesemakers would also have known each other.

The two men had finished the cheesemaking season on November 27 and had walked to Mount Horeb to collect their pay from their boss, Mr. Ragats, on Tuesday, December 11. Kuhni had received payment for one and a half months, as that was how long he had worked at this factory as an assistant.

On Wednesday, December 12, John Kuehni, age twenty-six, and William Christen, age thirty, returned from a hunting expedition. It was a beautiful fall day, probably one of the last pleasant days Mother Nature would give Wisconsin until the next spring. Squirrels were plentiful, and a rabbit or so for dinner was considered a treat. These men were accustomed to hunting for their meals, as they each had grown up in poverty.

The weather had dropped to nineteen degrees the night before, and it was going to snow and become much colder. Christen walked to the Holland residence, located to the south of the factory, where he purchased a loaf of fresh bread from Marion Holland. She was probably the last person to see him alive, except for John Kuhni.

After having supper, which they prepared themselves, they sat down and played a game of cards together, taking a drink (probably more) of alcohol as a pastime. John mentioned again that he and William were good friends and spent much time discussing biblical stories. This night John read out loud from his Bible about the story of David and his life as a king.

Christen had one obsession which was decidedly exasperating to John—that of ridiculing everything pertaining to religious matters. John would read from the Bible aloud in the evening after the supper hour, and Christen would laugh and sneer at the stories, language, and characters. John had been raised in a strict religious home and was a firm believer in anything written in the Bible. Thereby great differences arose between the two men.

On this particular night, Christen began to revile the Israelite king mentioned in the book and scoffed at many of his actions, holding the king up to ridicule. He began to call John a fool for believing any of that "nonsense," as he called anything related in the Bible.

He continued to rant and rave and then began calling John a liar and continued to heap insults upon him. John's anger began to rise, but all attempts to convince

Christen that the stories were true had failed. Christen continued the insults, and John could not stop him and became very frustrated.

After some time, John became weary of these insults, shut the book, as he knew he could not win the battle, and went to bed. Lying in bed, unable to sleep because of the insults to his religious beliefs, he continued to fume.

Soon William came to bed and asked John to indulge in another drink of whiskey to "restore peace" between them. Christen then disrobed and went to bed on the outer side of the small bed, which was pushed against the wall.

After Christen was asleep, John continued to think about his friend's evil, reflecting upon the wickedness of his mind and his actions towards the word of God. John grew more and more frenzied about what a bad person William had become since leaving Switzerland, as John knew he had come from a religious family.

Christen's lack of religion troubled John for some time, and he soon concluded that his friend's heart must indeed be black. If William could permit himself to talk as he did about sacred matters, he was undoubtedly destined for hell. There was no other way out for someone with a black heart.

Where did the term "black heart" come from? John might have heard the term from his father while being reprimanded for his "evil" deeds. Perhaps it came from the minister of the church he attended as he was growing up, or from his teacher.

The dictionary describes a black heart as belonging to someone or something innately evil or fundamentally corrupt. Across many cultures, humans have long believed the heart governed emotion, thought, and character—and was even the soul itself. The color black, meanwhile, has ancient associations with evil, evoking darkness, storms, decay, and death. Black-hearted, or "malevolent," doesn't appear until at least the 1630s. A black heart, specifically, emerges in records of the 1700s and 1800s, often describing a melancholy, hateful person with evil intentions.

Basically, "black heart" or "black-hearted" is likely a description of someone's cruelty or mean-spiritedness.

Our ancestors had no medical understanding of the function of the heart and the circulatory system, but they did understand that in the heart resided the love of God and the Holy Spirit. Probably some of the thoughts rushing through John's mind as he contemplated what to do were: "Why am I such a bad person? I read the Bible. I love everyone—and yet I do things, terrible things that hurt my family and myself.

"William is the best friend I have ever had. He is the only one who has shown some compassion for me except for my mother, and she is too far away from me and has no power anymore to help me. The rest of my family will have nothing to do with me, even my brother and his family."

Craving for someone to care for him, John loved this only friend he had at the time, and he evidently felt persuaded to help Christen. But how could he do this? Somehow, he knew the heart had to be removed from the body in order to save the soul. Had he read this somewhere, or did his conscience tell him what to do? He knew with his limited comprehension that he must remove this black heart from his friend's body; the soul could not enter heaven with a black heart attached.

But in order to remove a heart from a human body,

the body would have to die. Then the evil part that was poisoning the body could be removed. The more he thought of it, the more convinced he became that such a wicked creature as Christen ought not to be allowed to live with such a heart, as he would not be allowed to enter heaven.

His story continues:

About 10 p.m., he crawled from the back of the bed, where he was lying, over his partner, and out into the room where the stove was. Here he seized a stick of wood with a bulky, sharp knot on one end and returned to the bedroom. From the light of the stars shining through the window, he could plainly distinguish the face of his comrade lying on the pillow. He deliberately raised the bludgeon and, without hesitation, brought it with terrible force down upon the forehead of Christen.

The latter was awakened and sprang up with a cry of pain and anger. He attempted to defend himself, but the weapon came down a second time upon his skull, and he dropped back onto his pillow. A third blow felled him to the floor, where several more put an end to his earthly existence.

What did John think as he watched the lifeblood flow from his friend as he lay dying? What could possibly have gone through his mind? We will never know.

"Alone…
Long I stood there wondering, fearing, doubting,
*   dreaming dreams, no mortals ever dared to dream before…"*

—Edgar Allan Poe, "The Raven"

When did John come to his senses and begin to recognize what he had done? Probably once the alcohol wore off. Later he told his lawyers and his doctors that he was not sorry he had done this crime at the time, because he knew there would be no hope for Christen to enter heaven with a black heart attached to his body.

The only thing in his mind at the time was that he had to do it, and he went about doing it with certainty; he could not consider anything else at the time.

His story continues:

John then grabbed the body and dragged it down the stairs to the cellar. He had all the time in the world, no one was watching, and he began to disassemble Christen like a piglet.

With the ax, he cut off the head, and then, taking his jackknife, began to mutilate the remains for the purpose of seeing if his victim's heart was indeed black.

He succeeded in removing that organ and asserted that it had, in reality, begun to turn black. He was now reassured that what he had done was right. He was glad he had killed him; else, there would be no hope for Christen in the next world.

I wonder when John began to debate the rightness of his actions in his mind. But at some time during the night, John's mind must have told him: "Someone is going to find out about this; I have certainly done wrong!"

There must have been conflicting emotions. One was that he had done the right thing by saving his friend, and the other was knowing he would now have to face the public and the fact that he had committed a crime. But what could he do at that point? There was no way to put the battered body back together again, no way to replace the blood and tissue. John had to regain some control over the situation, and he tried in the only way his immature mind allowed him to.

∽

Back to the Courtroom. All through the morning, Mr. Rufus Smith continued to read the story related to him by John on November 11, 1889; reporters scribbled frantically as macabre detail piled upon detail. Every eye in the room was on the prisoner as the story became more and more gruesome. Every so often, Smith would suddenly stop, take a long breath, and then continue on with the story.

John continued his mutilation by removing the lungs and other organs. He placed the body in a sack. He described taking this sack about three-quarters of a mile south to a road running west from the Primrose post office, and there dug a grave and buried it. The heart he buried in another place several rods from where he interred the body. He buried the heart separately from the body because he said he knew that if the heart should go to hell, the body would be safe from such a fate; according to his mind, the two had to be separated.

He described to me, in great detail, how after burying the heart, he knelt down and prayed that the body should be mercifully dealt with in the next world. He also prayed that, if he had done wrong in killing Christen, his God would be merciful to him.

The head, liver, and other organs were put in another bag, weighted with a rock, and thrown into the Sugar River, where they were found by the Rea brothers twelve days later. John described in detail how he spent Thursday cleaning up the traces of his crime as best he could, and on Friday left the county, going first to Monroe to purchase a ticket to the old country on the Lord Gough.

Listening very carefully to Smith's telling of his story, John remained calm. But, as the day passed, his face gradually turned ashen and very pale, and he slowly began looking very troubled and much older. As he listened to the graphic detail of all—or nearly all—of the story of that night, I wonder if he hadn't hidden away from himself some of the horrors of those long hours. Certainly, no one could remember all the graphic, horrible details that were being told to the court that day.

❧

This, in substance, is what he confessed, but this confession had not been made until the Sunday before the court was called in November, almost one year after the deed, hence the necessity of asking for further continuance and investigation of the case. The council did not quibble or delay the trial on mere technicalities but did what their duty demanded their client. When his story was told to the physicians, they said that a reasonable time ought to be given them to determine his condition with a special examination of John's case. They later told how as they listened to his horrible and bloodcurdling confession, they found it hard to believe he was telling the truth. After conferring with each other, they agreed that perhaps John's imagination was running wild, that he had lied in his first confession. Surely all of this could not be true.

But, as there was no one who could verify if his story was true or not, the physicians felt compelled to rely on John's words. After a long, careful, and untiring study of his case, they concluded that while he was what might be termed a "moral monstrosity," he was still responsible for his acts.

Psychiatrists interpret mental states and emotional needs through a patient's demeanor and confessions of feelings and behavior. The physicians had satisfied themselves that John was responsible for his actions at the time of the crime, and in view of the overwhelming circumstantial evidence, he had been advised to plead guilty. Between the doctors and the lawyers, they were convinced this was the only and best way for John. He must plead guilty. And he did!

The expense of a jury trial had been averted!

❧

The report was written a little differently in the *Gogebic Iron Tribune* of Hurley, Wisconsin.

The reporter wrote:

Kuhni's story shows that the crime was a horrible one. It was told with a view to show that he was a religious fanatic and that his crime was committed while laboring under religious excitement. He told of how, prior to that day, Christen had ridiculed John's religious beliefs and laughed at him for reading the Bible. After being laughed at again that night, John had killed him with blows from a log and then decided to determine if indeed the heart was black. So, he cut off the head, opened the body, and removed the vitals, leaving the body there until the following night.

The heart was buried in one place, and the other parts were carried and buried about a one-half mile away from where the heart was buried. The head and other vitals were placed in a sack and thrown in the creek.

This reporter further determined that John's lawyers were convinced John was insane, and that the story had been fabricated to strengthen the plea.

Chapter Nineteen
Final Statement

To the defense lawyers, John was neither a statistic nor a component of a legal procedure they had undertaken to correct. John was their client, and it was their job to see him acquitted. When the odds mounted against this outcome, they began to try their best to present him as unstable or mentally unable to reason.

Found in the January 16, 1890 issue of the *Wisconsin State Journal* is the account given by Rufus Smith, the Dane County lawyer, to the court:

The condition of this man's mind has been carefully considered by many men in whose judgment courts and juries must have high confidence, and to whose opinion we must attach a great weight. We acted, as we believe, in accordance with our bound duty in securing time for this defendant, in which this matters this vital question, could be carefully investigated. This investigation has been made, and the attorneys for the defendant—I may say, your honor, Judge Siebecker, as well as Mr. Harper and myself—are thoroughly satisfied that, there is something about this man's mind that is not right; that he is mentally unsound to some extent, peculiarly constituted, that he is not built as other men are built.

While we are convinced of these things, we are equally well convinced that the borderline between responsibility, which at times is extremely vague, unsatisfactorily and hard to find, had not been crossed by this defendant; that he was responsible in the law for the commission of this crime. Having been thus convicted, we have followed our duty, we think, in advising this man to plead guilty.

With this confession before the people of the county, there will be not one person, it is thought, who will declare there were no reasonable grounds for the delay of trial. The lawyers for the defense are entirely exonerated from any improper motives in asking and receiving a continuance, but as a result of their effort and with but little additional expense to the county the physicians have satisfied themselves that Kuhni was responsible for his actions and accordingly, in view of the overwhelming circumstantial evidence, he was advised to plead guilty.

Henceforth, the expense of a jury trial at the adjourned term was averted.

⤜

Court Continues:

After a few minutes, District Attorney Erdall says to the prisoner—"Do you plead guilty or not guilty?"

Kuhni, in broken English, very quietly, barely over a whisper, says—"I plead guilty."

After a long moment's pause, Judge Bennett, one of the pleasantest gentlemen to ever occupy a bench in the state, speaking in the most Christian-like manner and with deep feeling, addressed the prisoner as follows:

Court—"Do you understand when you plead guilty to this charge of murder in the first degree that it becomes a verity that the duty of the court is to sentence you to state's prison for the rest of your life?"

Defendant—"I understand that the court has the power to do that."

Court—"The court not only has the power to do it, but it is the duty of the court to do it—a duty, which the court cannot shirk, but must perform."

Defendant—"Yes."

Court—"It has been since I have been on the bench, one of the saddest duties I am ever called upon to perform to sentence someone to the state prison for life, particularly a young man just entering upon the opening period of life when everything in his life has been pleasant and apparently his prospects fair for happiness and usefulness.

"There is something implanted in the breast of every human being that teaches him that murder is wrong. One of the Ten Commandments promulgated by Moses, written on tablets of stone more than fifteen hundred years ago, is, 'Thou shalt do no murder,' and the Christian world from time immemorial has prayed, 'Lord, have mercy on us, and incline our hearts to keep this law.' This commandment has not only entered into the law of every civilized nation that speaks English, but it has become the law of every nation that has a written language and printed laws. This is for the purpose of human life conceded by all civilized people, to be just.

"You have violated and taken the life of your fellow countryman—one, I understand that you were living and sleeping with at the time you committed the murder.

"I understand that you came here from Switzerland, a Christian country, and a country that has produced a

brave and generous people as there are on the face of the earth. You had only been here a very brief time—I understand not over a year, in this country when you committed this crime. Then after committing this murder, you, like the first murderer of which history gives us any account, fled from the justice of your country to another across the ocean.

"But as it turned out you could not escape this—the result of your crime; the recollection of that was awfully and fearfully present with you all the time, and you could not escape it, and you have been brought back here for the purpose of trial, and you have pleaded guilty and thus saved the county the expense of a public trial.

"However poor a person may be in this country, however unfamiliar with our law, the law, in its mercy, does not permit any person to suffer punishment for any crime, however grievous it may be, until he has first been convicted either by a trial on his behalf or his own plea of guilty. Had I not been informed that you had counsel, I would not have received your plea of guilty until I had appointed counsel to confer with you.

"Upon your plea of guilty to the information, the court now finds and adjudges you guilty of murder in the first degree, in the manner and form as charged in the information. You will now, of course, be committed to the state prison of this state for life."

Court—"Have you any mother living?"
Answer—"Yes"
Court—"And a father?"
Answer—"Yes."
Court—"Brothers and sisters?"
Answer—"Yes, sir."
Court—"Are they in the old country or this country?"

Answer—"One brother lives in this country and four brothers and two sisters in the old country."

Court—"The crime, which you have committed and for which you must suffer must have fallen upon your father and mother and your brothers and sisters with crushing weight, and I hope it may be some gratification to them to know that you have been fairly dealt with by the courts of this country, in which you are a stranger. And although you must go to the state's prison, you will not be cut off from all social privileges. You will have the benefit of attending church there, where you can think over and repent of this crime, of which you stand convicted upon your own plea of guilty. And I can only hope you make the best possible use of the privileges that are still left to you."

Then the mighty instrument, the gavel, struck by the judge at that moment, sounded like the tolling bell of a magnificent gothic cathedral. Even if the prisoner should have been acquitted, he would never forget its awful sound as it struck the judge's bench that day.

"John Kuhni, the sentence of the court is that you, John Kuhni, be punished by confinement in the state prison at Waupun, at hard labor for the term of your natural life from today noon, at 12 o'clock; and that the first two days of your confinement in state prison be solitary; and that on the 12th day of each December (the anniversary of the crime) during each and every year of your confinement in state prison, your confinement be also solitary. You may be seated."

Then arose a cry from the prisoner, a sound that was a half-cry, like something wounded, ashamed, and angry.

He could be heard to say, "Take me away from this place so that I may not be looked upon any longer."

At this point, Mr. Harper, the leading lawyer appointed to John, asked to be heard. "I think, perhaps, it may be due to the prisoner that a few words are said for him in reference to the crime, and I would ask the court to listen to a statement from my cohort, Mr. Smith."

The judge replied, "I will hear it, but nothing can be said that will affect the punishment I have to inflict."

Mr. Smith rose to address the court:

"I am aware of that," replied Rufus Smith, "and the few words that I may say, I say at the request of the defendant. It would be much more congenial in my feelings, if his honor, Judge Siebecker, who was removed from this case by his appointment of judgeship, could have said these words, as he has had charge of the prisoner during these past few months, and has been present with him almost day and night."

Smith continues:

It occurred to me that a word may be said in relation to the case, in view of the great interest that has been manifested by the public in this prosecution, and the appalling nature of the crime, which the defendant has committed if you look at it in a certain view of the case.

When we took charge of the case, we found to our surprise that this defendant was not by any means a brute and was not a man that seemed to have very many brutal instincts and characteristics we naturally look for in persons who commit great crimes. Instead, we found a man that seemed to have a keen intelligence, bright and tender susceptibilities, a man of sympathies, and tender feelings. The court perhaps noticed when the reference was made to his mother, it brought tears to the eyes of the defendant, and the counsel has seen him at other times to show deep concern and strong emotions.

We also found that this man had killed his best friend, his warmest friend, in fact, the only friend he had in this country, and he did it under such circumstances that there did not seem to be any adequate motive. It could not be said; the consideration has forced itself upon us, that it was for the purpose of gain because there was but a small amount of money there anyway; he knew beforehand what it was and where it was. He had abundant opportunity to take the money and get away with it in the repeated absences of William Christen if that has been his motive.

There was no intimation that these two men at the time were of the influence of liquor, at least to such an extent as to account for the commission of the crime. There was no evidence that they had any quarrel strong enough for the attack.

In view of all these circumstances and in the absence of any motive, and in view of the character of this man, the court can see that the question as to his mental condition, the state of his mind, was an inquiry that addressed itself to us with great force; and it has been the subject of much anxious investigation on the part of the attorneys for this defendant.

It did seem to us that the only way to account for the commission of this crime at all was by supposing that there was something abnormal or wrong about this man's mental constitution or that he was laboring under some temporary delusion, and for that reason, during the spring and summer after his apprehension, the subject of the condition of his mind was a matter that forced itself upon his counsel with great weight, and much time and labor was spent in trying to solve that problem.

We could not get much assistance from the defendant because, for purposes of his own, he entirely denied the offense, and we were led to do the best we could. Judge Siebecker accordingly corresponded with people in the old country who knew the defendant during his boyhood. Just before the commencement of the November term of this court, something came to the knowledge of the attorneys, which seemed to demand more investigation. It was then learned for the first time to the certainty that this defendant had actually committed the offense of which he was charged; that is, that he actually did the killing, and the circumstances under which it was done were for the first time brought to the knowledge of the attorneys representing this defendant, and it then transpired beyond all question, that this defendant killed Christen in what he says he thought to be religious zeal, and everything in the previous and subsequent history of this man, that we have been able to get hold of, fortifies and strengthens that opinion, which has become a conviction in the minds of the attorneys of the defendant.

After another long pause, Smith continued:

I believe that he killed Christen under a certain sense of duty at the time.

He killed him believing that William was a bad man and that he ought not to live; he killed him, killed his best friend, there in that solitary cheese factory, feeling at the time that it was his solitary duty to do so.

And on knowing these things and feeling the great weight of this responsibility as we did, we did insist upon a postponement of the consideration of this case until that matter could be thoroughly and carefully investigated, and this has been done to the best of our abilities.

While we are convinced of these things, we are equally well convinced that the borderline between responsibility and irresponsibility, which at times is extremely vague, unsatisfactory and hard to find, had not been crossed by this defendant; that he was responsible in the law for the mission of this crime.

Having been thus convinced, we have followed our duty, I think, in advising this man to plead guilty.

I say these words because—(pause followed by a long sigh)—I think they are due to this defendant. I think it is due to him that the people of this country may know these facts, that they may think of this defendant with as much kindness and consideration as is possible under these circumstances.

I think that it is also due to him to say—(another pause)—if the sheriff will permit me to say it for him—(pause)—that during his confinement in the local jail, he has been a model prisoner, kind, courteous, and obedient. He has spent the larger portion of his time reading from his Bible, along with other religious literature, and his mind would seem to have bent in that direction. He has evidently done his best to behave himself.

I think he now fully realizes—(pause)— the enormity of the offense of which he has been convicted, and I think he is going from here to the penitentiary in a better state of mind that he has been for months.

He is going there with the deliberate resolve of being as good a man as he can—(pause)—he tells me so—of being obedient to all the rules. He is going with deep remorse for the crime he submitted to his very best and only friend, and I hope that notwithstanding that, for this crime, he spends the remainder of his life in that facility and that through its walls there may yet come some rays of sunshine upon his head.[17]

Smith then took his seat. Smith was later once described as "a human digest of legal knowledge." He later became Dane County circuit court commissioner, holding the job for fifty years.

Mr. J. L. O'Connor, the assistant to the D.A., arose to address the court:

"I have been employed to assist Mr. Erdall in the prosecution of this case against Kuhni, and in my opinion, no unnecessary delay had been indulged in by delaying the trial." He went on to say that some people had made statements to the contrary, but that was because of the nature of the crime and a lack of understanding of the case and the defendant.
The judge made a few more statements regarding the case and then remanded John to prison before departing the room along with Sheriff Vernon.

------

[17] *Madison Daily Democrat,* 17 Jan. 1890

Chapter Twenty
A New Home

After Smith's statement, there were probably a few people in the room who felt at least a little sorry for John—especially those who had worked with him the previous year. John was a man who appeared outwardly to be like you and me. However, no one in the courtroom broke down in tears as a human being was condemned to life in prison. Perhaps his mother, living in Switzerland, would have shed tears had she been in the room. Kuhni was led away by the guards, and no one there felt it should be any other way. The only thought that went through any mind that day was, "This man was and is still evil."

So, the last chapter of the atrocious murder of William Christen, which took place more than a year before, had now ended. It took eleven months to break John into a confession. He was a stubborn man, and he held steadfast to his original story, although it altered a few times. It was time, along with the convincing evidence found by his lawyers, that finally convinced him it was useless to hold on to his story any longer.

John was taken that afternoon from the courthouse to his future home behind the walls of the state prison at Waupun, Dodge County, and given the prisoner number 3602.

The horror was over, and John was secured in prison,

but the atrocious murder lingered in the minds of Dane County citizens for a long time. It was described in *The Story of Primrose 1831-1895*, written in 1895 by Albert O. Barton, and published by Mary Zumbrunnen, as "the great and exciting trial of the season." Two columns recounted the tragedy.

Barton writes:

"The worst crime that ever stained the soil of Primrose was the murder of Cheesemaker William Christen, by John Kuehni, in December 1888."

The author stated that the Holland Cheese Factory was built between 1875 and 1880 to serve Amund Holland, his brother Ole Holland, and Elling Eielson's farm. After the crime, the factory became known as the "Murder Factory."

The story relates much of what I have written previously, but there are several inaccuracies in his version: Barton says John did the deed because of money, which was proved wrong, and many of Barton's facts regarding what happened to Christen's body are incorrect.

The story is also told in a very short form in *Wisconsin Death Trip* by Michael Lesy.

Chapter Twenty-One
A Final Note

The long days in prison would have weighed heavily upon John, prisoner number 3602, and soon his courage would have begun to wane. Depression, despair, and loneliness would cause him to sink into desolation and the loss of his health. There was no escape. He had been caught, and the evidence against him was compelling.

After serving six years, John passed away at the state prison in Waupun on December 2, 1896, of tuberculosis, or TB at the age of 34. He was buried in Forest Mound Cemetery in Waupun. The custodians carried him to the little prison cemetery located at the back of the prison grounds. Number 82 marks his grave. Did the prison superintendent say a few prayers over the body before placing him in the ground in a common wooden box? No one will ever know. Probably not. [18]

TB is a contagious, infectious disease, and was considered to be a death sentence at the time. It was most commonly spread by breathing in infected droplets put into the air when someone sneezed, coughed, or spat. The

---

[18] Wisconsin State Prison Records

bacteria can spread from the lungs to other parts of the body to cause tuberculosis of the lymph nodes, bones, brain, and throat, for example. A lowering of the immune system due to overcrowded housing, mediocre food, and stressful conditions can create particular susceptibility to this disease. John would not have received much in the way of treatment, which the disease demanded. [19]

Prison records at Waupun provide a physical description showing a scar on each side of Kuhni's nose and one on the back of his head. The documents also listed that he had a brother, Fred Kuehni, of Primrose, Dane County, Wisconsin.

They also state, "His physical condition is not good; his mental condition is good. His complaints during his confinement were of weak eyes, consistent cough, heart trouble, neuralgia, and lots of colds, sour throats, and debility." These conditions were documented up to December 31, 1895, almost one year before his death. Nothing is listed for his last year.

Located outside Waupun in the township of Chester, the Forest Mound Cemetery was the final resting place for unclaimed inmates from the Wisconsin State Prison (now Waupun Correctional Institution) and patients from Central State Hospital. It was used from 1871 to 1975.

Initially, each grave had a marker bearing the grave number. In the 1980s, metal markers were installed bearing the name, number, institution, and date of death

---

[19] Daniel, Thomas M. (2000). *Pioneers of Medicine and Their Impact on Tuberculosis*. Boydell & Brewer.

of each individual. Those markers were later replaced with one large sign bearing the names and dates of death of those buried there. The sign was later removed for repairs. The graves are currently unmarked. The persons listed are from Wisconsin State Prison unless otherwise noted.

⁓

The death of John Kuehni was evidently of no concern to anyone in the area where the murder had been committed, as the local *Belleville Recorder* on the day following his death listed only an item about Ole Skuldt of Primrose, who was selling five wagonloads of hogs in Verona and receiving $4.20 a pound for them. There was no mention of the death of the Horrible Dane County Murderer.

Were his possessions offered to his brother, Fritz? Probably, but nothing has ever been found that belonged to John that Fritz's family has ever known of. Apparently, no one in the family even wished to claim his body or his few possessions. I find it unusual that not a single photo has been found of John; however, we do know that one existed and was in his hands when he was captured in Ireland.

Did anyone mourn his death? I think not. His father had died in December of 1892, and his mother died in October of 1893, both shortly after his imprisonment. His brother Fritz was probably very much relieved that he did not have to feel sorry for the brother sitting in jail for the rest of his life. I suspect Fritz anguished much over the murder and spent time speculating and trying to understand how someone in his family could possibly do what his brother had done.

However, Fritz was going through a very stressful time of his life during these years. Three months after his brother was committed to Waupun prison, he and Paulina had another child named Jacob, who was born on April 24, 1890. A daughter, Anna, followed shortly in November of 1893.

Then, in 1895, tragedy struck. Fritz's wife of twelve years died suddenly on April 14 at the age of thirty-three. It must have been trying for Fritz, left alone to raise four small children. He would have had little time to concern himself with a brother in prison located many miles from his home. Fritz remarried to Elizabeth Losenegger on May 22, 1896. John died in prison in December of that year.

Another brother, Samuel, living in Switzerland when the murder occurred, married while John was in prison, and in 1893, Samuel and his new wife emigrated to Wisconsin along with a nephew, Gottfried, and Gottfried's wife. Did either of these men visit John in prison once they reached Wisconsin? I am sure they did not, as they were very embarrassed by his deeds and were not about to forgive him in any manner; they wanted only to forget about him and be over with the horror. They, like John's father, had no patience for someone with mental problems; John must endure his punishment, including abandonment by family.

Chapter Twenty-Two
Explain This Guy

Now, how do we explain this guy, John Kuhni?

He is now dead. We will never exactly know what went on in the mind of John Kuhni the night of the tragedy; we can only speculate as to what he was thinking at the time, and rely on what he told his doctors, lawyers, and the court.

As I read and reread the articles, I began to form an image of this person, someone I have never met. If John was not insane, then what was he? Why did his beliefs turn him into a killer?

John had to be at least a little short on common sense, judging by the way he attempted to cover up his foul deed. Any normal person would have buried much of this evidence instead of leaving it to be found; there was a lot of wild forest land nearby to easily cover his crime. A normal person would not have worn the clothes belonging to the victim or taken personal items of his victim, especially all the way back to Switzerland. There were many other acts following the murder that a sane person would not have done, such as throwing body parts in the creek.

With John, insanity was foremost, but behind that were old-world customs. John barely spoke English, and his mind and heart were still in the closed, tradition-bound village of his childhood. His ancestors were of the peasant population that depended on agricultural lands rented from wealthy owners. Swiss peasants were persistent, inventive, and stubborn as they carved out a simple life in that mountainous country. Even today, the expulsion of winter, along with its evil spirits and demons, forms part of the local tradition in the mountains of Switzerland.

Coming from a society of rules and deeply held beliefs, John sincerely believed in God. Early lessons taught him a sensitivity to good and evil. Christians do believe that Satan can enter our minds and influence our behavior. Are these people mentally ill? No. A false belief is not necessarily mental illness. He just took his religious nature and carried it to the extreme without realizing the gravity of the law and what he was actually doing.

Switzerland was basically a conservative world. Faith and old customs helped the family father maintain his authority as if he were a king with his court ("a man's home is his castle"). Religion was a sacred heritage, and useful in training the younger generation in the difference between right and wrong. The family father rejected the hotheadedness of youth with its revolutionary ideas (just those opposed to his own). He looked to keep his wife and children under a firm hand and would not stand for any insubordination.

The line separating religion from superstition can be indistinct, especially during the years John was growing up. People who commit these kinds of horrors usually come from unhappy childhoods, perhaps caused by an absent or abusive father. Perhaps the mother blamed the child or clung too tightly to the child because the father was abusing him. Such a child soon learns the power of violence. He has never witnessed the love between parents and knows only punishment.

An article in the *Janesville (Wisconsin) Daily Gazette* of January 17, 1890, tells me:

...that Kuhni committed the murder because Christen laughed at some bible stories appears to have no foundation. ...It seems that he once attacked his father on a highway in Switzerland and robbed him of his money.

This is the first time I have heard this information. Where did the writer get it? Probably from interviewing the lawyer or one of the doctors treating John. It could be true, as he was found guilty of stealing in Switzerland several times.

What about the unthinkable act of mutilation? This was not a religion, but something from the old world. John believed deeply in the magic of the old world. John feared magic, witches, and devils. He was known to carry rabbits' feet in his hip pocket as a protection against these evils. People did accept pagan gods, demons, and superstitions.

His low intellect was evident to his family while he was growing up, and probably little discussed among his siblings. However, his father probably degraded him whenever he could for not being normal. Through the years, his father, and possibly his brothers and school friends and minister, all helped to bring about his deep feelings of worthlessness.

When he was sent to America, abandoned by his family and country, the judgment of his lack of worth had probably destroyed any self-respect he once had. The abandonment of a dependent child is terrifying because it symbolically means death, and John was still a child in a man's body. The truly dependent cannot survive without those that support them. One wonders how many other people John destroyed when he raised that block of wood and caused it to come crashing down onto William's skull.

I wonder what would have happened if John had buried all of the body instead of throwing part of it in the river, only to be found within a week. No one would have looked for either man for several weeks, and by that time, John could have been in Switzerland. He would have eventually been caught, but the story would have played out a little differently.

Was the final verdict fair? I personally feel that John's closing statement was the truth because it fits with the evidence. It was at first thought that he had carried parts of the body in the satchels on his trip to Switzerland, but they were filled only with wet clothing that he had tried to wash out. Because of the cold weather, the clothing did not dry, thus making the bags heavy. That would account for the liquid that resembled watery blood. Because of his past and present state of poverty, he could not bear to part with any clothing of good quality, whether it was his own or someone else's. He could not comprehend that taking the clothing would condemn him; the thought never came to him.

It was not for the money. He had ample time and opportunity to steal money from Christen without killing him but had not done so.

The crime was defined as a cold, calculated, and "monstrous" murder. The lawyers and doctors declared that John had not presented himself as a monster.

I believe that alcohol had a lot to do with John's behavior that night. Evidently, the amount of alcohol consumed that night (and I believe he had more than was recorded) was too much for John's already small brain. It is known that alcohol steers a person's mind away from common sense, and he had the brain of a small child, to begin with.

Also, a normal person could handle someone defaming his religion; John could not. He truly believed that what he was doing was right and that he had to remove the corroded heart from the rest of Christen's body in order for his friend to gain entry to heaven. However, his brain could not tell him how to do it legally. He was living with the mind of a little boy in a big boy's body.

In 1888, individuals were held responsible and answerable for their actions. Unless he was indeed "insane," the presence or absence of mental illness was of little interest to the courts. According to the law, men who were not insane or idiotic were expected to control their evil passions, violent tempers, or brutal instincts, and if they did not do so, that was their own fault; they must suffer the consequences.

Even today, those people who are most obviously crazy are rarely acquitted on insanity pleas, especially when their crimes capture public attention and involve open trials. Some crimes are so atrocious that the jury, like the public at large, will not hear that the individual is insane. Those that come to mind are Sirhan Sirhan, David Berkowitz, Richard Speck, the Manson family, and many others. Today, the real crazies will not come to trial despite all the evidence.

Compare John's case with another, from 2003, in which a jury cleared Robert Durst of Galveston, Texas, of murder. He had definitely chopped up his neighbor and tossed the pieces of the body into Galveston Bay. He used two saws, an ax, a box of plastic garbage bags, and a bottle of Mr. Clean.

Durst was reported to have accidentally killed his neighbor, and the jury ruled it an accident. It was irrelevant what he did after the death; he had tried to cover up the deed under a haze of alcohol and panic. Defense attorneys recounted Durst's turbulent life, including his mother's fatal plunge from a rooftop when he was seven, the disappearance of his first wife, and years of chronic alcohol and drug use. After hurling the bags into the bay, Durst had paid the rent of his victim so the landlord would not notice he was missing. Yet he got off!

There is no doubt in my mind that if John had gone to court today, or even a few years later, he would have been placed in a mental institution where he might have lived out the remainder of his natural life. His story compares somewhat to that of Wisconsin's Ed Gein, though Gein murdered and robbed graves for his own satisfaction.

However, during my extensive research on John and the occurrence of the murder, I find him not to be a serial killer. This was a one-time, poorly thought out, violent way of trying to save someone he cared for in the only way his limited mind could conceive.

At the time of the murder, he was in a religious, superstitious, and compassionate state of mind. His feelings of worthlessness, depression, and abandonment, and his lack of anyone to discuss his feelings with, combined with an underdeveloped mind fueled by alcohol, caused him to believe he had to do the necessary repair work for his friend.

Conclusion

Today, 130 years after this horrible event, the creek still runs past where the cheese factory once stood. The building is long gone, but the leveled area against the hillside shows where it once stood.

For years, the remains of the basement could still be seen, but they are slowly disappearing into the ground, taken over by weeds. A well on this spot has been dynamited to fill it in.

The creek begins only a few rods to the north of this spot, fed by an underground spring; it twists and turns toward the east and the Sugar River. This area still floods each spring over a thick layer of hardpan that holds the water above it. Throughout the years, the farmers who owned this land have tried everything to prevent the flooding, even dynamiting, which did help for a while. However, Mother Nature is persistent, and it remains a swamp surrounded by farmland.

Throughout the years, many local young people, especially the girls, have dared each other to sit in the basement area where the factory once stood and watch for ghosts. None were ever seen. At least none have been reported.

The "Murder Factory," as it was later called, was built between 1875 and 1880 to serve Amund Holland's 160-acre farm, and was constructed between two brothers' barns, which stood ninety rods apart. In 1888, the cheese factory was located between the houses of A. S. Holland and John Gruening; both owned the building at that time.

After the murder, the factory continued to operate, with John Schingler and his wife, Barbara, as operators. After ten years, John hired a younger cheesemaker to help him manage the business. In 1908 the factory was closed, and the local farms began hauling their milk to the Oak Grove Factory on the southeastern corner of Section 9. The land was later sold in three pieces, one each to John Groening, John Anderson, and Olin Hanna.

❧

To members of the Kuehni family,

I did not research John Kuehni's story and write this book to please the readers, but to learn and to bring forward the truth. You may take it or leave it, but the facts are accurate as far as I could find.

A few questions for you:

- Should I have even attempted to turn up the facts in this horrible family tale? I could easily have ignored the story and written my family history without the interruption of a not-so-perfect family member, but then you would not have had the chance to read about John. So, I will leave the answer up to you:

- ***Should I have*** sanitized this story?

- Did I flesh out this skeleton in my family? Did I make it dance for you?

Appendix One
More Information About Dane County & the Local People Involved in the Story

Primrose Township

Primrose Township, where the cheese factory was located, was just north of the New Glarus area, where throngs of Swiss immigrants first settled. Fritz Kuehni, cheesemaker and farmer, had settled among the Scandinavians west of the area, where the next generation of Kuehni's would settle near Belleville and Verona in Dane County. Later, this became a dairy-farming area.

Christen Family

I have never been able to learn much about the family of William Christen, and I have never found a marked gravesite for him. I do not think any descendant will ever know where to place a monument to mark his remaining bones. It is strange that there was never a memorial service held for him, no death certificate, or any other record.

A Wilhelm Christen, born in Switzerland in 1860, arrived in this country on April 13,1885, at the Port of New York. On the ship's passenger record, he listed his occupation as farmer, and he arrived alone. This is probably the William in my story.

I did find a John Christen living in the township of Primrose in 1885. There was one male in the family and two females. Previous to that, in 1880, a Samuel Christen, age twenty-three, lived at Adams, Green County, and worked in a cheese factory. He was single and lived with Karlen Godfrey, who also worked in a cheese factory. Both were born in Switzerland. I found Samuel living at or near New Glarus in 1900, age forty-five, born in Switzerland, immigrated in 1879, and married in 1883 to Anna. They were parents to John, age sixteen, and Samuel, Jr., age fifteen, and six younger children.

This could be a brother of William Christen, who was killed in 1888.

In 1900, Edwin and Peter Christen, ages one and two, lived with their grandparents John and Barbara Shingler in the township of Primrose, very near where the murder took place.

There was an Albert Christen who lived near Waterloo, Wisconsin, with Swiss roots. His parents, Jacob and Elizabeth, had emigrated in 1854. There was also a Jacob Christen, born in 1873 in Switzerland, who lived in the Auburndale area. He had learned cheesemaking from his father. But he did not come to Wisconsin until 1893.

There is also a record of a Reverend O. P. Christen living in Angelica, Wisconsin, in 1899. He was a Methodist minister.

Fredrick (Fritz) Kuehni

Fritz Kuehni was the first Kuehni relative of mine to emigrate to America. Fritz and Paulina married at Koppigen, Switzerland, on December 1, 1882, and sailed to America in 1883, settling near other Swiss families at New Glarus. The first group of Swiss immigrants to settle here was from the canton of Glarus, not from my family's home area of Bern. Fritz certainly would have known some of the later settlers.

In 1888, Fritz lived at a factory called the Peterson Cheese Factory, later known as the Standard Cheese Factory. The children would have attended the Hannah School in Section 16, which was later called the Primrose Center School.

Fritz lived a hard and tragic life. His first wife passed away, leaving him with many small children. He lost a son, Jacob, at the age of seven to unknown causes, and another son, Jacob, at age eighteen to consumption, as it was called at the time, or tuberculosis, a disease of the lung. At the time, there was no cure for the disease. After Fritz remarried, his first son, born to his second wife, passed away at birth. Worst of all, he lived through the embarrassment of having a murderer for a brother, years of headlines in the local newspapers, and many court trials.

Leaving southern Wisconsin for northern Wisconsin at the age of fifty-nine had to be especially hard on his health. He became blind at the age of seventy-five and lived to the age of eighty-four—a miracle, given what he had lived through, and testimony to the sturdiness of one Swiss man.

Holland (originally Haaland)

The Holland family came to Primrose in 1854, settling in Section 16. The sons of the family arrived with their stepfather, Rasmus Jacobson Dalen, and lived with the Jacob Jacobson family. Syver/Sever became a teacher. Several boys served in the Civil War, with Sever acting as drillmaster. He later became the Primrose town chairman in 1869 and justice of the peace. Sever passed away in 1884, before the murder occurred.

Amund Holland, a son, purchased a 304-acre farm from Knute Nelson, Ole, and Sever Holland, adding adjoining acres until the family owned a total of 440 acres in Sections 9 and 16.

Eli Pederson

Eli was very active in Primrose Township activities.

Peter O. Baker

Peter, after many years as town chairman and elected to the Wisconsin Legislature as an assemblyman.

Ole O. Barton

Barton was the clerk of Primrose at this time and town chairman.

Knut Peterson Myrland

Myrland came to Primrose Township with his parents in 1854 and purchased 240 acres in Section 21, and Knut, his father, purchased land in Section 20. He died in 1895.

Rea Family

George and William Rea were sons of John and Ellen Rea, originally from Scotland, who settled in Section 10 in Primrose. John could play the bagpipes and was a stonecutter. He helped build the Hanna Schoolhouse in Section 16.

Martin Hobbs

Hobbs purchased the John Rea family farm in Section 10 in the late 1860s and taught at the Mount Vernon School in the 1880s.

John Tascher

John Tascher, of Swiss origin, married Anna Elmer, also of Switzerland. He purchased land in Sections 4, 5, 8, and 9. The family made Limburger cheese and helped to organize the Primrose Union Cheese Factory Association in 1878. The factory was built in 1878 just below their house near the road and burned down in 1898. A new factory was built in 1902. John served on the Primrose Township Board and Dane County Board of Supervisors.

Hoesly Family

Henry and Elania Hoesly were born in Switzerland; their son Mark was born in Wisconsin in 1860. Henry purchased the Peter O. Baker farm in 1887, and another farm to increase his holdings to 295 acres by 1890.

Jacob Hoesly, born in 1880, took over this farm, called the Valley Stock Farm, before 1900. He married Rosina Becker, and the couple had two sons, Clarence and Clifford. Jacob farmed until 1946.

Rufus Smith, Lawyer

Rufus Smith, Dane County lawyer, was once described as "a human digest of legal knowledge." He later became Dane County circuit court commissioner, holding the job for fifty years.

Governor Rusk

Jeremiah McLain Rusk (June 17, 1830 - November 21, 1893) was a U.S. Representative, the fifteenth governor of the state of Wisconsin from 1882 to 1889, and the second United States secretary of agriculture from 1889 to 1893. Jeremiah was a farmer, soldier, and politician who commanded the 25th Wisconsin Infantry during the Civil War.

His most noted act during his governorship was when he sent the National Guard into Milwaukee to keep the peace during the May Day Labor Strikes of 1886. The strikers had shut down every business in the city except the North Chicago Rolling Mills in Bay View. The guardsmen's orders were to shoot to kill if the strikers attempted to enter the Mills. But when the captain received the order, he ordered his men to pick out a man and shoot to kill. This led to the Bay View Tragedy, in which a number of workers were killed. Governor Rusk took most of the blame.

In 1889, after the end of his third term as governor, he accepted a cabinet position as secretary of agriculture in the Benjamin Harrison administration.

John Erdall

John was elected district attorney for Dane County for one term from 1888 to 1891, and in 1895 became assistant attorney general for Wisconsin. In 1901 he became an attorney for the Chicago Great Western Railway.

J. J. Tschudy

Tschudy was the ticket agent in Monroe, and J. J. Tschudy, from 1846 to 1855, handled the business and spiritual functions of the church for the early Swiss immigrants who settled in or around the Colony of New Glarus and later held many public offices. Tschudy was the first Swiss person to be voted into office in Green County, first as a recorder, later as registrar, and then as county clerk. There were many Tschudy families among the very first Swiss settlers, and the first doctor to practice in New Glarus was a Mr. Tschudy, whose father was a doctor in Switzerland.

Works Consulted and Interviews

Madison Daily Democrat, Wisconsin State Journal, and *Milwaukee Journal* Newspapers

Wisconsin Magazine of History, Spring 2005

History of Dane County, 1880

Dane County death inquests

Dane County Circuit Court Records, Film #A211

Wisconsin State Prison records

Cheese: The Making of a Wisconsin Tradition by Jerry Apps

Establishment and Development of the New Glarus Colony: 1884-1892 by D. Durst

Remote Origins of the Kuney (Kuehni) Family, Willey Blake article

New Glarus by Kim D. Tschudy

Wisconsin Death Trip by Michael Lesy

Various obituaries

Newspaper clippings

Freitag, Duane interview

Remy, Jerry interview

Judd, Willard interview

Anderson, Ken interview

Sinclair, Mary in conversation with the author, May 21, 1996.

Lambert, E. R. testimony

Parker interview

About Atmosphere Press

Atmosphere Press is an independent, full-service publisher for excellent books in all genres and for all audiences. Learn more about what we do at atmospherepress.com.

We encourage you to check out some of Atmosphere's latest releases, which are available at Amazon.com and via order from your local bookstore:

Rags to Rags, nonfiction by Ellie Guzman

Heat in the Vegas Night, nonfiction by Jerry Reedy

Evelio's Garden, nonfiction by Sandra Shaw Homer

Difficulty Swallowing, essays by Kym Cunningham

A User Guide to the Unconscious Mind, nonfiction by
    Tatiana Lukyanova

To the Next Step: Your Guide from High School and College
    to The Real World, nonfiction by Kyle Grappone

Breathing New Life: Finding Happiness after Tragedy,
    nonfiction by Bunny Leach

Love Your Vibe: Using the Power of Sound to Take
    Command of Your Life, nonfiction by Matt Omo

Letting Nicki Go: A Mother's Journey through Her
    Daughter's Cancer, nonfiction by Bunny Leach

About the Author

Betty Plombon, an avid historian and genealogist, is always in search of a good dead man! She is the author of *Katrina and the Forgotten Gulf Coast* and several local history books.

The founder of several Wisconsin historical and genealogical societies, Betty has given many talks on both subjects to local, county, and state workshops and other groups. She has made seventeen research trips to Salt Lake City, attending weeklong classes while doing research on her family lines and for other people. She retired as President of the Chippewa County Genealogical Society after 17 years including acting as newsletter editor. She helped raise that society from an infant to a very successful organization with a wonderful research library. She was secretary and newsletter editor and board member for the Chippewa County Historical Socicty for many years. After raising five children, today she is the museum director and newsletter editor for a very successful museum in Stanley, Wisconsin. A relentless worker, she believes in pushing herself and others along to do each job right, while maintaining a sense of humor.

Betty is a native of Stanley, Wisconsin, and now resides in Diamondhead, Mississippi. She returns to Stanley each summer where she spends her spare time at the museum building exhibits, researching and writing stories for the society's newsletter and programs, all while helping others to research their family histories. She is also writing many of her own family histories, which will soon be available.

She loves to read, research, write, garden, and play bridge.

Visit Betty on her Web Page: Betty's World at bpwritingworld.com. She loves to hear from you.